THE MYSTERY OF THE WILL OF GOD

Colombia para Cristo video introduction

Martin, that mountain is a mess.

Watch the La Montaña trailer, a film based on a true Stendal event

THE MYSTERY OF THE WILL OF GOD

A Message to the Persecuted Church

Russell Stendal

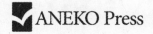
ANEKO Press

www.lifesentencepublishing.com

Visit Russell's website: www.cpcsociety.ca

The Mystery of the Will of God – Russell M. Stendal

Copyright © 2014

Printed in the United States of America

First edition published 2013

LIFE SENTENCE Publishing books are available at discounted prices for ministries and other outreach.

Find out more by contacting us at info@lifesentencepublishing.com

LIFE SENTENCE Publishing, ANEKO Press
and its logos are trademarks of

LIFE SENTENCE Publishing, LLC
P.O. Box 652
Abbotsford, WI 54405

Paperback ISBN: 978-1-62245-049-7

Ebook ISBN: 978-1-62245-050-3

10 9 8 7 6 5 4 3 2 1

This book is available from www.amazon.com, Barnes & Noble, and your local Christian bookstore.

Cover Design: Amber Burger

Editors: Sheila Wilkinson, Ruth Zetek

Share this book on Facebook

To my wife, Marina, and to the wonderful family that the LORD has given us.

House and riches are the inheritance from fathers, but the prudent wife is from the LORD. (Proverbs 19:14)

More books by Russell Stendal

Contents

Preface

Over the past fifty years many pastors, friends, and even fellow missionaries have died in Colombia for the cause of Christ. Some of the graves are located in the little cemetery at our Lomalinda radio station; others are scattered across the length and breadth of this great nation.

According to the United Nations, we now have almost six million displaced persons, most of whom are Christians (Roman Catholic or evangelical). The most common story is that they have lost their homes, farms, livestock, and livelihood simply because they refused to participate in the ongoing, dirty war. Some refused to continue to be involved in kidnapping, drug cultivation, atheism, spiritism, or other forms of corruption, so they were distrusted and mistreated by those on all sides of the conflict.

The Lord has a handful of others who have remained at their posts through thick and thin. For reasons known only to the Lord, we have been like John and Philip while some of our friends have been like Stephen and James.

This book is a compilation of seven spontaneous messages given before a live audience. We have beamed these messages on dozens of radio stations (including international, shortwave coverage) to the persecuted church located in remote rural areas of Colombia and along its treacherous borders with Venezuela, Peru, Brazil, Ecuador, and Panama. This is a small sample of almost one thousand similar messages that we have produced over the past fourteen years.

A central theme that repeats itself in our messages to persecuted Christians is that God is in the business of bringing the types, shadows, and symbols of the Bible and those depicted in many religious rites and ceremonies into reality in the life of the believer. This reality is the bride of Christ. Jesus is the Head of a body of Christ with many members. He will soon return for a bride without *spot or wrinkle or any such thing*.

What started out in the New Testament as "love feasts" or "agape" in memory of our Lord and the communion of his Last Supper, has now dwindled to a few drops of grape juice and some cracker crumbs in many congregations. As early as Genesis 14:18, bread and wine have been symbols of the Melchizedek covenant. Jesus, the real king of righteousness, is the High Priest and only Mediator of the new covenant, the priesthood of all believers according to the order of Melchizedek (Hebrews 5; Psalm 110:4). Wine is the symbol of his life, and Jesus said the bread is his body that is broken for us (1 Corinthians 11:24). It is to his broken body, the persecuted church, that these messages are directed.

Ephesians 4

15 *but following the truth in charity, let us grow up into him in all things, who is the head, the Christ:*

16 *From whom the whole body fitly joined together and well tied together among itself by the nourishment that every connecting bond supplies, by the operation of each member according to [the] measure they have received, making increase of the body unto the edifying of itself in charity.*

I wish to acknowledge those whose footprints I have followed in search of the truth (Song of Solomon 1:8). The truth, of course, is Jesus the Good Shepherd. It was my friend Dr. C. R. Oliver who introduced me to the Song of Solomon. My godly parents, Chadwick M. Stendal and Patricia C. Stendal, raised me in the fear and admonition of God and set the stage for everything that was to follow. Other outstanding mentors include Clayt Sonmore, Ray Rising, George Warnock, Buddy Cobb, and countless others.

I have enjoyed following the footprints of great heroes of the past such as Martin Luther, Casiodoro de Reina, William Tyndale, John Wesley, Hudson Taylor, C. T. Studd, George Müller, Oswald Chambers, and C. S. Lewis.

May these messages be of great encouragement to anyone suffering trials, tribulation, or persecution *Until the day breaks and the shadows flee away* (Song of Solomon 2:17; 4:6).

– Russell M. Stendal

CHAPTER 1

Draw Me ... Let Us Run

Let us run with patience the race that is set before us.
(Hebrews 12:1)

*Let us be glad and rejoice and give glory to him; for
the marriage of the Lamb is come, and his bride has
made herself ready.* (Revelation 19:7)

This bride is a helpmate compatible with him. They are of
the same nature. This is seen in the Song of Solomon. She
is not the woman clothed with the sun of this world (Revelation
12:1). She does not use the gifts, anointing, and ministry given
by the Holy Spirit to obtain the things of this world as personal
gain or to control the work of God with *the moon under her feet.*
She is not crowned with the twelve stars of human leadership
that have been gifted by God for a time and a season. She is
clothed in fine linen which represents the Sun of Righteousness
and the direct work of God in and through her (Malachi 4:2).

> 8 *And to her was granted that she should be arrayed
> in fine linen, clean and bright: for the fine linen is
> the righteousness of the saints.*

She knows the difference between self-righteousness and

his righteousness. She will not be found ashamed or naked on the day described by the prophet Joel when *The sun and the moon shall be darkened, and the stars shall withdraw their shining* (Joel 3:15).

The new day that follows is described by the prophet Isaiah:

Isaiah 30

25 *in the day of the great slaughter, when the towers shall fall.*

26 *Moreover the light of the moon shall be as the light of the sun, and the light of the sun shall be sevenfold as the light of seven days, in the day that the LORD binds up the breach of his people and heals the stroke of their wound.*

29 *Ye shall have a song, as in the night in which the Passover is kept and gladness of heart as when one goes with a flute to come into the mountain of the LORD to the mighty One of Israel.*

30 *And the LORD shall cause the power of his voice to be heard.*

The people of God in the Old Testament were symbolized by the moon because they did not have the indwelling presence of the Holy Spirit. Now God's people can shine like the Sun of Righteousness. This is not a reflected light. It is light that comes from within as a result of a change in nature. This is a woman (people) of the new creation. This is a woman who is compatible with the Lord Jesus. Then the new day of the Lord will shine seven times brighter than anything we have ever seen.

Revelation 19

9 *And he said unto me, Write, Blessed are those who*

DRAW ME ... LET US RUN

are called unto the marriage supper of the Lamb. And
he said unto me, These are the true words of God.

Anyone who participates in this supper feasts on the true words of God. Now the Word will go forth with more force, and this will lead to a new generation where the sons of God (regardless of gender) are multiplied and enter into a blessing that we have not had until now.

> *The wine of the cup of communion with the Lord is death to one thing and life to the other.*

The Song of Solomon is the history of the formation of this new bride. Where did she come from? How does God deal with her? How is she led? What are the stages of growth and maturity that she must pass through before she becomes by nature everything that God desires?

Song of Solomon 1

1 *The song of songs, which is of Solomon.*

2 *Oh! if he would kiss me with the kisses of his mouth! for thy love is better than wine.*

This is a woman who desires intimacy with the Lord, and wine is a symbol of life in the Scriptures, life of the Lord, or life of the natural man in the flesh (which provokes the wrath of God). The wine of the cup of communion with the Lord is death to one thing and life to the other. This is the process of new birth; this is the process of death and resurrection. She prefers his love over her own life (wine). This is what makes her qualify. This is not a person who says, "I love him because I know he can give me what I want; because I know he can bless me here in my fallen nature." She is seeking him with all her heart and she desires to enter into his eternal life instead of trying to get him to descend to her level. This is very important.

3 *Because of the savour of thy good ointments*

— 3 —

*(ointment poured forth is thy name), therefore have
the virgins loved thee.*

Ointment is anointing oil and symbolizes the nature of
God. There are two parts to this. One is the human who in
his natural state can be "anointed" and function in representing God while retaining the nature of Adam and Eve. This is
how the church has functioned until now, but to be victorious
we must enter into the very essence of his being. This woman
desires to be like him and exclaims:

4 *Draw me after thee, we will run.*

Now we see a different situation. Orders are given to the
slaves and to the servants, but the bride is different, even when
she is just beginning to be wooed. This applies to each of us
as individuals. Even though the bride of Christ is made up of
many members, the Lord treats each of us as unique. He does
not give the bride brusque orders. He draws her with invitations.
Servants are given orders, but we do not do this to our friends.

This is why we do not organize people into ministries and
divide them into groups – children, youth, young couples,
women, men, seniors, jail ministry, hospital visitation, etc. No,
things do not function in this manner. They function by free
will. Not by my will or by your will but because we volunteer
to be drawn by him. He does not order us to go with him – it
must be of our own free will. This requires incentive on our
part to go beyond a normal walk – we will run.

4 *The king has brought me into his chambers; we
will be glad and rejoice in thee; we will remember
thy love more than the wine; the upright love thee.*

You may think that this relationship with the king is pro-
gressing too fast. She desires to begin the nuptial relationship
with kisses and enter into the chambers of the king. Who knows

what will happen there? This is a pure and clean love that only the upright can understand, but the person whose heart is not upright is disqualified from even beginning this relationship.

> 5 *I am dark, O ye daughters of Jerusalem, more desirable as the booths of Kedar, as the tents of Solomon.*

She claims to be dark (the original says *burnt*). The sun of this world burns, and she has been burnt by the world. She knows from painful experience about the attraction to the dangerous things of this world. This is what makes her so desirable to him, for the Lord is seeking those who have been burned by this world and are willing to admit it. They may seem very dark to others, but to the Lord they are beautiful.

> 5 *as the booths of Kedar, as the tents of Solomon.*

Here is history: Kedar is of Ishmael, the son of Hagar, who represents the old covenant. *Solomon* (meaning "peace offering") is a type like Sarah, who represents the new covenant. *Sarah* means "princess." This woman must come out of the old and enter into the new. She must receive a new name and nature. At first she is sterile, and the Lord must deal with her, for her own vineyard is not fruitful:

> 6 *Do not look upon me because I am dark because the sun has looked upon me; my mother's sons were angry with me; they made me the keeper of the vineyards, but I have not kept my own vineyard.*

This woman is still in the system, still in the church as we know it, burned and beat up by the world. Even so, she did not seek her own glory. She sought the good of others. Now she is embarrassed and self-conscious as the king looks upon her.

> 7 *Tell me, O thou whom my soul loves, where thou dost feed, where thou dost make thy flock to rest at*

noon; for why did I have to be as a wanderer after
the flocks of thy companions?

The flocks of the companions receive everything secondhand. Someone who has a personal relationship with God has a flock, but that flock serves that person, who is not God, even though he claims to know God. This woman has wandered after those flocks (from church to church) but she wants a direct relationship with the king; she desires to be fed directly from him. She has been confused, yet has this tremendous desire inside. She is sterile and has a desperate desire to bear good fruit.

She wants to be singled out. She desires rest. She has some qualifications that are not readily apparent and does not think she has much of a chance, but here comes the reply:

8 *If thou know not, O thou fairest among women,*

What happened? She really got his attention! He is looking at her heart, and he sees unbelievable beauty.

8 *go forth, following the footprints of the flock and feed*
thy little female goats beside the booths of the shepherds.

She is receiving a tremendous authorization, but first she must follow the footprints. What footprints? There are so many men and women of God who have gone on before, or are in front of us, and have left a good example. They have left footprints. Where do the footprints lead? They lead to the Good Shepherd. The true ministry of evangelism is to be able to say with Paul, "Follow me, as I follow Christ." For if we are following Christ and others follow our tracks, they also will find him.

He is giving her instructions. She is not shepherding sheep but goats. She is pasturing those who have not been born again, those who do not have the new nature. She is frustrated.

How often must a schoolteacher teach children like this? But if she does this out of a good heart filled with faith, these little goats (kids) may come to know the Lord, and he may replace disorder with order.

In reality, the flocks of the "companions" of the Lord, who have no direct contact with the Lord and the "sheep," are not encouraged to have direct contact and are not really sheep. They are mostly goats. For the sheep know his voice and will not follow the voice of a stranger. In the Old Testament, the word for small cattle could mean sheep or goats, and under the Law they could sacrifice either. In the New Testament, however, a judgment separates the sheep from the goats.

> *She is pasturing those who have not been born again, those who do not have the new nature. She is frustrated.*

The next verse sums it up:

> 9 *I have compared thee, O my love, to a mare of the chariots of Pharaoh.*

Two things: *O my love* means that she is a friend and no longer a servant. The Lord said that he does not share his intimate plans with servants, only with his friends (John 15:13-16). He is now ready to share intimate things with her. The courtship is serious.

She knows she has captured his attention and she is a candidate for what he seeks. But some adjustments must be made in her life, and she must be tested. No man is going to marry without assurance that she will be faithful and represent him the way he desires because the woman is the glory of the man.

A mare of the chariots of Pharaoh is a compliment. She is extremely beautiful to him. However, she is hitched to the wrong chariot. Pharaoh is the god of this world.

Brother Clayt had a dream in Colombia. He saw an old-fashioned, elegant horse cart with a terrible woman as the passenger, whom he understood was Jezebel. She was stunning in a certain sense, but she was very domineering with a lot of religious machinery and a little driver sitting in front wearing a horrible mask. Behind the mask was something even worse because the driver was the Devil. Two beautiful white horses were hitched to the cart and were traveling all over Colombia. Clayt saw this dream three times.

The Lord showed him that there are very special people who have a heart for God but are hitched to the wrong cart. They are hitched to the religion of men, which is really the cart of Jezebel with the Devil driving. These well-meaning, naïve people are making an all-out effort but are duped into spreading abomination.

A mare of the chariots of Pharaoh is beautiful, talented, and hardworking but is hitched to the wrong purpose. Scripture speaks of a horse that the Lord will ride to battle. He is calling us to be that horse, the one he rides to victory. This scene is described in Revelation: One who is faithful and true (Jesus) rides a white horse to victory with all the armies of heaven following (Revelation 6:2; 19:11-14). Jesus desires a woman who is not only part of him but also a projection of him. He desires someone who will not use him to get what she wants; he needs her to be transformed. He has many options and chooses not to condemn her. He will draw her, so he says:

10 *Thy cheeks are beautiful between the earrings,*
thy neck between the necklaces.

11 *We will make thee earrings of gold with studs of silver.*

She is wearing what looks like jewelry, but it is not exactly to his taste. Her jewelry is really the harness to Pharaoh's chariot! And she feels proud and pretty in her splendid attire. But he is offering her another class of jewels. *We will make thee earrings of gold.* What are earrings of gold? They are the capacity to hear the voice of the Lord. Gold is the divine nature which will be placed in her ears with studs of silver. Silver is the symbol of redemption. He wants to accomplish her redemption and arrange things so she only hears his voice.

If she will leave the harness of the chariot of Pharaoh, she may receive golden earrings with studs of silver. He will redeem and deliver her from all the "wonderful" things that she is doing. He knows that she has been pulling that chariot with good intentions. He knows that the ministry she has with the little female goats is a wholehearted effort. But this is not what he has in mind for his bride.

12 *While the king was on his couch, my spikenard gave forth its fragrance.*

The word *spikenard* occurs only five times in Scripture – three in the Old Testament and two in the New Testament. It means "total, loving, surrender." This is what was in the alabaster box broken by the woman in Mark 14:3 when she poured the ointment over Jesus' head. This was the response from a woman who was willing to sacrifice everything.

Judas was annoyed and complained that the spikenard should have been sold and the money given to the poor, when in reality he wanted it to go into the bag of funds which he managed and had been dipping into. Scripture mentions many tests and trials, but when the spikenard gives forth its fragrance, this is hard to miss. Jesus said, *Wherever this gospel shall be preached throughout the whole world, this also that she has done shall be spoken of for a memorial of her.* Why?

This woman anointed Jesus for burial by giving him everything while he was still alive. She represents the bride. Other women anointed Jesus after he was dead. These others are the bridesmaids. Nicodemus also came through after Jesus died. Many like him will qualify to be friends of the groom.

The bride qualifies with everything. She holds nothing back.

When the king redeems her from the harness of the chariot of Pharaoh and places golden earrings with silver studs in her ears, what does she do? She breaks the alabaster box that represents all her gifts and abilities. This is to become a living sacrifice. This is a peace offering (the meaning of *Solomon*) that ascends with a pleasing odor to the throne of God. She continues:

> 13 *A bundle of myrrh is my wellbeloved unto me*
> *that rests between my breasts.*

Myrrh is a symbol of the cross. The bride knows that to embrace her beloved is to embrace the cross. The Ishmaelites who bought Joseph from his brothers and sold him into Egypt were merchants who sold myrrh. Myrrh was also one of the ingredients that made the beauty of Queen Esther surpass all the other maidens. Nicodemus took some to the tomb. Myrrh was one of the gifts of the wise men. It has a delightful smell but is very bitter. The bitterness of the way of the cross eventually brings forth its delightful, breathtaking odor.

The bride knows that to embrace her beloved is to embrace the cross.

It is clear that she understands the way of the cross. When she breaks the alabaster box and embraces the myrrh between her breasts, she knows beyond a shadow of a doubt that she is going to travel the same path of persecution, humiliation, and victory as her beloved. She embraces him of her own free will. He is not ordering her to do this. He is inviting her. He is not manipulating her with guilt trips. This is completely voluntary.

This is different from the slaves and servants who must obey orders and from those who turn to God in a foxhole situation after exhausting all other options. Although she may have started out in one of these situations, she is a capable woman with much potential. She chose to take care of the vineyards she was charged with at her own expense. He looked on her, called her, and showed her the footprints of his flock that she was to follow. She is willing to follow, and he offers a change if she allows him to redeem her from the service of the chariot of Pharaoh and listens only to him. She surrenders everything, even what she considers to be her good gifts and abilities, and understands the full implications of the way of the cross. The bundle of myrrh rests between her breasts, and she receives a revelation that is ongoing. Peace and rest come when she embraces the way of the cross. She gets a glimpse of his plan and purpose.

> 14 *My beloved is unto me as a cluster of camphire*
> {Heb. ransom} *in the vineyards of Engedi.*

Camphire is used two times in the Song of Solomon, but in the rest of the Scriptures it is translated as *ransom*. She understands that he gave his life for her. The vineyards of Engedi are a wonderful symbol. Engedi is part of the inheritance of Judah, and the lawgiver shall not depart (Genesis 49:10) from that tribe, the Lion, from which the Lord Jesus descends. In the end of the book of Ezekiel, Engedi is where the fishermen fish. This woman has been fished for, and now she is receiving revelation like Paul of being able to do *all things through Christ who strengthens me.* With her beloved, she will inherit the ability to fish lost souls into the kingdom and nurture them with the wine (life) of the Lion of the tribe of Judah who will write his laws on the tablet of their hearts and in their minds.

He continues to build her up with *revelation in the knowledge of him* and with words of edification so she will follow him anywhere.

> 15 *Behold, thou art fair, my love; behold, thou art*
> *fair; thou hast doves' eyes.*

The dove is the symbol of the Holy Spirit. He tells her that she has the capacity to see things from God's perspective. She understands the gospel and can see by the Spirit; this is another reason she is so fair in his eyes.

16 *Behold, thou art fair, O my beloved, and pleasant.*

She does not see him as far away or difficult. His personality is being imprinted in her. When the brothers of Joseph went to Egypt, they thought that the lord of Egypt (their brother) was terrible, when in reality he was bursting with love for them – love which they were not ready to receive because they did not understand the gospel.

16 *also our bed has flowers.*

17 *The beams of our house are cedar, and our rafters of fir.*

Cedar does not rot. Insects cannot eat it. It is a wood that resists corruption. Fir speaks of being upright. Now she can see that she is part of a house (household) that will not rot nor be corrupted. Even the bed has flowers. New life, new gifts, and creative beauty are springing forth.

She started out shepherding some little goats (kids). Scripture says the Word comes forth we know not how, first the blade, then the flower, then the fullness of the fruit (Mark 4:28). The fruit is what God really wants. This bride is delighted with the flowers. There are flowers in the realm of the Spirit of God. She has the Holy Spirit and can see with the eyes of a dove. She can see the flowers. Soon there will be fruit. When the fruit comes and if it is what he is expecting, there will be a tremendous reaction in him.

If what he does produces a certain response from us, there are things he is yearning for and expecting. When they come forth in us, the reaction from him is more than we can describe with words. She starts talking about flowers and a house that will not be corrupted and look at the response from him!

Song of Solomon 2

1 *I am the lily of the field* {Heb. Sharon} *and the rose of the valleys.*

2 *As the lily among thorns, so is my love among the virgins.*

He says that he is that flower, the lily, from which the costly and precious spikenard is extracted. She and the other virgins who seek him are compared to roses (extremely beautiful but they have thorns). This implies that there remain in them aspects of the old nature that must be dealt with. Lilies have no thorns.

3 *As the apple tree among the trees of the wild, so is my beloved among the sons. I desired to sit under his shadow, and his fruit was sweet to my taste.*

She is directly under his covering and is being fed with his fruit. This will produce great changes in her. The apple tree is important because later there is another reference to the apple tree that completes the picture (Song of Solomon 8:5).

But where did our problem begin? Did it not have to do with an apple? With the wrong apple, all it took was one bite for us to lose all hope and for everything to be ruined. Now, this is a very different apple tree. It is not the Tree of the Knowledge of Good and Evil but the Tree of Life. He, the Lord Jesus, is the tree of life. The fruit of this tree effects great redemption. It will produce a complete change in our nature if we continue to sit under its shadow (covering) and continue to eat of its fruit until we are producing the same fruit.

The river of God, which flows from the throne of God in Revelation 22:1-2, is also described by Ezekiel where there is not just one tree but also an entire forest of trees along the banks of the river (Ezekiel 47:7, 12). These trees will give their fruit in every season, and even the leaves will be used for the healing of the nations.

We are now beginning to understand what the Lord plans to do with this woman. The Lord is capable of doing this with each and every one of us, but he is seeking something in us. He is seeking a bride who desires to receive him in fullness. He is seeking those who are not seeking their own gain but desire to serve others. He is seeking those who can see things from his perspective, and this is only possible with pureness of heart (Matthew 5:8).

Let us pray:

Heavenly Father, we thank you for your Word which can cleanse our hearts so we may have the eyes of a dove, so the gifts of your Spirit may flourish in our lives, and so we may be compared to the lily which is your Son, Jesus. May we continue until the fruit of righteousness is produced in us.

We thank you, Lord, for giving us the opportunity to partake of the fruit of the tree of life after you effect your great redemption in us that we may produce this same fruit. We ask, Lord, that this will become a reality in our lives – that we may come forth out of the realm of being clothed with the sun of this world, out of the realm of being hitched to the chariot of Pharaoh, and enter into the realm of the woman clothed with the fine, white linen of holiness as your work is accomplished in and through us. May we qualify to be the bride without spot or wrinkle or any such thing. We know this is your work, but it also requires our disposition. We ask this in your name. Amen.

CHAPTER 2

Sent Ones – God's Definition of a Missionary or Apostle

And the witnesses laid down their clothes at a young man's feet, whose name was Saul.

And they stoned Stephen calling upon God and saying, Lord Jesus, receive my spirit.

And he kneeled down and cried with a loud voice, Lord, impute not this sin to their charge. And having said this, he fell asleep in the Lord. (Acts 7:58-60)

This young man named Saul is none other than the one who was later converted and became the apostle Paul.

In Acts 6, the multitude of disciples had named seven men as deacons (servants) to wait on tables and minister to the widows and others being cared for by the new believers. The first on the list was Stephen and the second was Philip.

We are not exactly sure how long Stephen waited on tables caring for the widows, but within a few verses it says, *And Stephen, full of faith and power, did great wonders and miracles in the people.*

His preaching left even the most prepared Jews without an

answer, so they did the same thing to him that they had done to the Lord Jesus: they put up false witnesses and had him killed.

After the death of Stephen, two interesting things are narrated: (1) Philip began doing what Stephen had been doing; and (2) God touched Saul who was leading the campaign against the Christians by persecuting them, putting them in jail, and killing them. The death of Stephen opened the door for these things to happen.

Many were converted under the ministry of Philip, and after Saul became Paul, even more were converted under his ministry. We see a progression, and we also see that in order to fulfill the purpose of God, unity was required. Since that time, one of the most efficient enemy strategies has developed. If the enemy cannot overcome Christians with a frontal onslaught, he will seek to join, infiltrate, and produce divisions and separate sects that do not get along with one another.

Acts 8

1 *And Saul was consenting unto his* [Stephen's] *death. And at that time there was a great persecution against the congregation* {Gr. ekklesia – called out ones} *which was at Jerusalem, and they were all scattered abroad throughout the regions of Judaea and Samaria, except the apostles.*

They killed Stephen and the same day attacked all the Christians in Jerusalem, who all had to flee except the apostles.

2 *And devout men carried Stephen to his burial and made great lamentation over him.*

3 *As for Saul, he made havoc of the congregation* {Gr. *ekklesia* – called out ones}; *entering into the houses and dragging out men and women, he committed them to prison.*

4 But those that were scattered abroad went every-where preaching the word of the gospel.

5 Then Philip went down to the city of Samaria and preached the Christ unto them.

6 And the people with one accord gave heed unto those things which Philip spoke, hearing and seeing the signs which he did.

> The demons seemed to be in the people who were the most religious.

7 For many unclean spirits, crying with a loud voice, came out of those who were possessed with them, and many paralytics and that were lame were healed.

8 And there was great joy in that city.

Samaria, like Jerusalem, was a religious city. When the Lord entered Jerusalem, one of the distinctive features of his ministry not only there but in all of Judea was that many demons came out of the people. The demons seemed to be in the people who were the most religious. The religion of Samaria was even more contaminated, such that when Philip arrived, many unclean spirits had to flee.

It happened like this: The Jews who did not receive the Lord attacked the Christians in Jerusalem, and all except the apostles fled. Those who escaped to different places, including Philip, began to give testimony of Christ, and the demons left and fled everywhere. The Jews scattered the Christians, and the Christians scattered the demons.

It is interesting to note that even when the ministry of Paul reached the Gentiles, there were fewer demons than there were in Judea, Jerusalem, and Samaria. These were places that supposedly had the truth. Today many groups claim to be Christian, and many apparently supernatural events are taking place. But sometimes when a person with discernment observes this, their conclusion is that much of this is not of God.

We went with Brother Clayt to speak in a large church, and after he spoke, they kicked him out. We soon saw that this was not the house of the Lord. They had another spirit, and when Brother Clayt spoke, all the unclean spirits began to cry out, even in the pastor.

> 9 *But there was a certain man called Simon, who*
> *before this in the same city used magic arts and*
> *amazed the people of Samaria, giving out that he*
> *himself was some great one,*
>
> 10 *to whom they all gave heed, from the least to the*
> *greatest, saying, This is the great virtue of God.*

What happened with Brother Clayt is what was happening in Samaria until Philip arrived with the real Holy Spirit. When the real presence of God was absent, Simon the magician seemed like *the great virtue of God.*

The people gave heed to Simon the magician, from the least to the greatest, until Philip arrived. In how many places do deceivers pass themselves off as great leaders when they sway multitudes by claiming their actions are the virtue of God? But if and when it really is the virtue of God, there will be the fruit of the Holy Spirit. When it is not the Holy Spirit, there may be many "wonder works" but no good fruit. The fruit will be the opposite; their fruit will be people full of hypocrisy seeking power and control with no scruples like the religious leaders of the Jews. They added to the Scriptures; they started endless meetings that God never ordered; they started synagogues that were never authorized by God; they built man-made temples that were never ordained by God, and they filled them with religious rituals that were never ordered by God.

There are examples of meetings in the Scriptures, but it never says that we must attend a meeting every Sunday or every Saturday; this is nowhere to be found. So, what happened? We have become conditioned because everyone has been doing these things for many, many centuries. It is true that the Holy Spirit can congregate the people. It is true that in the book of Acts there were meetings with many in attendance where someone preached, but these meetings are recorded because that was what God decided to do in a given moment in time.

On the day of Pentecost when Peter preached, three thousand were converted. This was not because someone passed out flyers, announced the meeting in the local media, and told people of the time and place where all the miracles would happen. Likewise, when Peter and John raised up the paralytic, they preached another message before a multitude in the temple, and many believed. But the message was interrupted when they had to answer to the supposed religious authorities and spend the night in jail. But God had them miraculously released, and they continued preaching the next day.

The message that Stephen gave, the one that caused his death, was not a message where someone planned to bring people together for a religious event. It was because the Jews were trying to bring down his ministry. They brought false witnesses and began a false trial. This turned into a big meeting with a message that is recorded in a long chapter in Scripture ending in the death of Stephen (Acts 6:8-7:60).

The messages of Philip in Samaria were not because the apostles and Christian leaders in Jerusalem had a get-together to plan and decide where and how to extend the work. That was not what happened. Something completely unexpected happened, and everyone except the apostles had to flee. Philip wound up in Samaria and continued flowing in what the Holy Spirit ordained for his life until the demons began to flee. His preaching had a great effect on all those who had been oppressed by the Devil. This was very different from many evangelistic campaigns that take place today.

Prior to his ascension, Jesus told the apostles to wait until they received power from on high. There has been confusion regarding the power that they were to receive. The word used indicates power under control. The Lord was not interested in unleashing rash, human arrogance out of control with gifts from the Holy Spirit. That which would come from heaven by the Spirit would also remain under the control of the Spirit.

Soon the servants who had been selected to wait on tables were doing signs, wonders, and miracles

We see something interesting here. The apostles were in the ministry, the ministry was multiplied into many people, and many were cared for in both the natural and in the spiritual realms: widows, orphans, people in need. Those who had excess sold their possessions and gave the funds to the apostles so no one remained in need. The apostles were dedicated to spiritual work and had many demands on their time. They decided to establish seven servants (deacons) to wait on the tables because there were complaints that the Greek widows were not getting the same attention as the Jewish widows. Note that it is amazing that they were caring for Greek widows as this would probably not have occurred to normal Jews. All of them had been touched by the Spirit of God.

They selected seven servants (*deacon* means "servant"), but Jesus taught that in the kingdom of God the least, who is the servant of all, is really the greatest. Soon the servants who had been selected to wait on tables were doing signs, wonders, and miracles, and were preaching with such unction that the

Pharisees and Sadducees who were attempting to derail the gospel were at a complete loss. Compare this to our day where individuals study in a fine place, and after four or eight years of study, they graduate and are then doctors of divinity, and they are called reverend (compare this to Psalm 111:9).

Those who were moving in the center of what the Holy Spirit was doing here were the disciples that Jesus chose. They became apostles when he sent them forth. The next group named in the Scriptures after the twelve apostles is the waiters; first the one, then the other, and we can be sure that many more followed because they *turned the world upside down.*

Not only this, but Philip arrived in Samaria where Simon the magician had duped the entire city. He had made them believe that he was grand and important, and that what he did with magic was really the virtue of God. How many Simons do we have in Christendom today? Simon let the cat out of the bag eventually because his heart was concerned with money above anything else. And when we see the modern Simons, they are always looking for money instead of sacrifice. They seek money but are not interested in risking their own lives for the gospel and for the Lord. So in the difficult places where it can cost someone their life if they mention the Lord, we do not tend to find a "Simon the magician." We find them where there is much money and where it is easy to influence naïve people with the supernatural.

Speaking of Simon the magician:

> 11 *And to him they had regard because for a long time he had amazed them with magic arts.*

Even today we have great places full of those who have been amazed for a long time and continue to be amazed at the spectacle of the modern Simons that appear to be the virtue of God.

> 12 *But when they believed Philip preaching the*

*gospel of the kingdom of God and the name of Jesus
Christ, they were baptized, both men and women.*

They were baptized after the unclean spirits fled, after the
demons left. Simon the magician was revealed for what he was,
because before that, everyone thought that he was the virtue
of God.

*13 Then Simon himself believed also; and when he
was baptized, he continued with Philip and won-
dered, beholding the miracles and signs which were
being done.*

The magic of Simon could not hold a candle to what Philip
was doing under the power of the Holy Spirit. Today many fill
large stadiums and do what appear to be great miracles, but if
we are to compare this with the real presence of God, it leaves
a lot to be desired. The true presence of God is very different.

*14 Now when the apostles who were at Jerusalem
heard that Samaria had received the word of God,
they sent Peter and John unto them,*

Samaria was not really Gentile. It was the residue of the
northern ten tribes of Israel that had been removed from the
land. Some had trickled back and mixed their beliefs with
other things, producing an even greater contamination than
those descended from Judah, Benjamin, and part of Levi who
continued to worship in Jerusalem. The Samaritans worshiped
in Bethel (which means "house of God") where Jacob (who
later became Israel) had sacrificed. The difference between the
Samaritans and the Jews was similar in some ways to our modern differences between Catholics and Protestants or Catholics
and orthodox Christianity. They had a common root, but over
time they had separated, and each contained its own leaven.
The only way to really cut through this is with the Holy Spirit
and fire. This is why Peter and John were sent.

15 *who, when they were come down, prayed for them that they might receive the Holy Spirit.*

16 *(For as yet he was fallen on none of them; they were baptized only in the name of the Lord Jesus.)*

In the Jewish world and in all that had to do with Israel from the books of Moses, if anyone recognized that they were unclean and contaminated, their remedy was to be washed in water. There were many ways to become unclean: You could sin or become sick; you could touch someone else who was unclean, or touch a dead body, etc. The spontaneous reaction of anyone finding himself in an unclean state was to seek the remedy described in the law of Moses. Many ways existed to become contaminated, but only one solution – wash in water.

This is where water baptism comes from. They knew that when the Messiah came he would find them all unclean. So the tradition said that when the Messiah came, they would all need to be washed. This is why they asked John the Baptist that if he was not the Messiah, why was he baptizing? So when Philip came to Samaria, the reaction was spontaneous; their way of manifesting repentance was the same as the Jews with John the Baptist. They got baptized in water but not in the Holy Spirit. Even though there were no dealings between the Jews and the Samaritans, both groups clearly understood the meaning of water baptism: it was a public declaration that they were not clean.

It is very sad that in the Christian era, even though almost all the different groups and sects have followed some form of water baptism, the significance for the most part has not remained clear. For many, it is simply a rite of membership into something, and they do not know and are not informed of the significance that this had for the Jews in the time of the New Testament. They know even less about the symbolism relating to the true gospel – that an old man must be buried so the resurrected Christ can live in us. Today there are many in the same straits as the Samaritans. They received the baptism in water and they came out wet, but the Spirit of God, the life of God, has not entered into them.

> *they came out wet, but the Spirit of God, the life of God, has not entered into them.*

Verse 17 speaks of what happened when Peter and John arrived in Samaria:

> 17 *Then they laid their hands on them, and they received the Holy Spirit.*

In this case, the Holy Spirit did not come by the water baptism. The Holy Spirit came when the apostles laid their hands on them.

> 18 *And when Simon saw that through the laying on of the apostles' hands the Holy Spirit was given, he offered them money,*

> 19 *saying, Give me also this power, that on whomsoever I lay hands, he may receive the Holy Spirit.*

Today we have something worse than Simon the magician. We have people who want to utilize a human method to confer gifts and ministry instead of depending directly upon God. You can go where these people are, and they sell you an expensive book or charge an entrance fee at the door so you can go into a room with several hundred people. The vast majority of these people do not know each other, but they are going to teach everyone to prophesy. They are going to pray for you, and you are going to become a "prophet." And just how do you prophesy? According to them, you just put your hand on the stranger standing next to you and say "good" things, and that is prophecy. Then they tell you that if you want your prophecies to actually come true, you have to come back, take a second course, buy another expensive book, and learn about apostles. To the degree in which you submit to your "apostle," your "prophecies" will come true, and this goes on and on and on. Not even Simon the magician would have done this.

> 19 *Give me also this power, that on whomsoever I lay hands, he may receive the Holy Spirit.*

> 20 *But Peter said unto him, Thy money perish with thee.*

Peter did not say, "Look, Brother, I do not feel that you are in perfect spiritual shape, but give us a nice offering, and I am sure God will bless you. Come with us, Simon, you clever magician, and share all that money you spent years collecting in this town and finance the Great Crusade of the Peter and John Ministries. We are the 'real' apostles. Just come along with us, and after a while, Simon, you will learn how we do things." This is not what Peter said. He said:

> 20 *Thy money perish with thee because thou hast thought that the gift of God may be purchased with money.*

> 21 *Thou hast neither part nor lot in this matter, for thy heart is not right in the sight of God.*

> 22 *Repent therefore of this thy wickedness and pray God, if perhaps this thought of thine heart may be forgiven thee.*

> 23 *For I perceive that thou art in the gall of bitterness and in the prison of iniquity.*

Peter did not say, "Look Simon, you don't understand. When a bad desire like this surfaces, you have to kneel down and ask for forgiveness. In fact, it is a good idea for you to do this every night because we all sin in word, thought, deed, and by omission. And if you confess your sins to the Lord Jesus, he will always be faithful and just to forgive your sins." Did he say this? No! He told him to repent and pray if *perhaps* this wicked thought could be forgiven. He told him that he was in the gall of bitterness and in the prison of iniquity. (Iniquity is when the person knows he is in sin and yet is trying to cover it up and pretend that he is fine.) Peter made him understand that God did not have to forgive him; God could decide to forgive or not to forgive. He scared the living daylights out of Simon the magician.

> 24 *Then Simon answered and said, Pray ye to the Lord for me that none of these things which ye have spoken come upon me.*

What could come upon him? Peter told him that his actual state was in the gall of bitterness and the prison of iniquity. But what Simon did not want to come upon him was God choosing to not forgive his wicked thought. This is implied in what Peter told him. There are not many preachers who would dare to say this to someone today.

> 25 *And they* [Peter and John], *when they had testified and preached the word of God, returned to Jerusalem and preached the gospel in many villages of the Samaritans.*

They did not speak again to Simon the magician. Simon was very frightened; we do not know what happened. We do not know if he really repented and if God forgave him. But later in the book of Acts, something similar happened. It looks like it was a different individual, but it might as well have been the same person. Paul had a problem with someone who was doing magic, and this person confronted him. Paul left this person blind, and everyone was aware of what happened (Acts 13:8-12).

Another interesting observation here is that Philip, full of the Holy Spirit, was preaching, and the demons were fleeing. So many signs, wonders, and miracles happened that even Simon the magician could see a huge difference between what Philip was doing and what he had been doing. But under the ministry of Philip, the Holy Spirit did not enter into the Samaritans. The Holy Spirit entered into the Samaritans when Peter and John came.

At this time, however, God sent Philip to another site, and his ministry was picking up momentum because the Holy Spirit was about to touch the treasurer of Queen Candice. Here we have several examples of how different people are baptized in {Gr. into} the Holy Spirit, and each example is different. In the case of Cornelius and his family, who were not even Samaritans, Scripture says this happened as on the day of Pentecost. Peter did not lay hands on them or even baptize them in water before they received the Holy Spirit.

When God dealt with Saul (Paul) in the next chapter of the book of Acts, Saul is blinded as the Lord Jesus revealed himself to him on the road to Damascus. God sent a disciple named Ananias who said to him (even though Saul was the worst persecutor of the Christians), *Brother Saul, the Lord Jesus ... has sent me, that thou might receive thy sight and be filled with the Holy Spirit* (Acts 9:17). Paul was filled with the Holy Spirit in a very curious way, which we shall examine in detail later. Apparently, Ananias was not an apostle (sent one), but he feared the Lord more than he feared man. So when God sent him, Ananias went and accomplished the work of an apostle.

God dealt directly with Saul, but he also incorporated those he desired to use. God used Philip when Philip fled to Samaria out of fear, and then brought Peter and John after Philip established a beachhead against the powers of darkness. God sent Philip and used Philip in the role of an apostle to the Ethiopian eunuch.

> 26 *And the angel of the Lord spoke unto Philip, saying,*
> *Arise and go toward the south unto the way that goes*
> *down from Jerusalem unto Gaza, which is desert.*

What happens when the Lord sends someone forth with a specific purpose? When the Lord sent his disciples who had left everything to follow him and then returned from their first journey, the Scriptures called them apostles.

Philip ended up in Samaria as the result of a great persecution. He and all the others fled, but the apostles did not flee because apostles are moved (sent) by the Lord. Apostles only go when God sends them. Those who were not apostles fled from the persecution. Even so, the Lord used many like Philip, and the gospel was spread throughout the region. The Holy Spirit spread, and the demons had to flee, and the apostles came to Samaria. But when the apostles arrived in Samaria, it says in verse 26 that *the angel of the Lord spoke unto Philip.*

This is interesting because the angel of the Lord spoke unto the prophets throughout the Old Testament. If we read through the book of Acts to when Paul was on a ship in the midst of a severe storm and no one knew what would happen (Acts 27), it appeared that all would be lost. Paul was able to calm everyone down by saying, "The angel of God stood by me tonight and told me this is what will happen."

Where is the angel of the Lord today?

> 26 *And the angel of the Lord spoke unto Philip, saying,*
> *Arise and go toward the south unto the way that goes*
> *down from Jerusalem unto Gaza, which is desert.*

What happened? The angel of the Lord sent him. And who is the angel of the Lord? The angel of the Lord represents the Lord and is like the Lord. The angel of the Lord is our Lord Jesus (to confirm this read Revelation chapters 1 and 10). The angel of the Lord sent him, and when the Lord sends, what happens?

The sent one is an apostle {Gr. sent one}. The Lord sent Philip to represent him. Scripture says that he who is faithful in little will receive more. Philip was faithful waiting on tables and look what God did with him!

> 27 *Then he arose and went, and, behold, a man*
> *of Ethiopia, a eunuch of great authority under*
> *Candace queen of the Ethiopians, who had*
> *the charge of all her treasure and had come to*
> *Jerusalem to worship,*
>
> 28 *was returning and sitting in his chariot reading*
> *Isaiah the prophet.*

A man of very high rank from a nearby country was returning to his home.

A copy of the book of Isaiah would have cost a small fortune, and the fact that he could read it in Hebrew was quite an accomplishment for a foreigner.

Many say that the Lord has spoken to them, but it is only the vain imaginations of their heart.

> 29 *Then the Spirit said unto Philip, Go near and join*
> *thyself to this chariot.*

The angel of the Lord sent him, and the Spirit told him to zero in on a specific chariot. Many say that the Lord has spoken to them, but it is only the vain imaginations of their heart. Philip had a direct encounter with the angel of the Lord, and the Spirit was fine-tuning the guidance along the way. There are many today who claim to be apostles of the Lord, but they have never been sent by the Lord. They may have been sent by a group. Maybe they did some studies, or they may have gifts that allow them to convince multitudes. Based on these factors, they have launched out. A true apostle, however, has had a direct encounter with the Lord. A true apostle has been sent by the Lord. An apostle cannot be set into place by men.

> 30 *And Philip ran there to him and heard him read the prophet Isaiah and said, Dost thou understand what thou readest?*

> 31 *And he said, How can I, except someone should guide me? And he besought Philip to come up and sit with him.*

How many are reading their Bibles every day? People have been taught that it is necessary to read a chapter every day or to do a plan that will get them through the Bible in a year. They are told which chapters to read every day. The most splendid plans have a chapter out of the books of Moses, a chapter of history, a chapter out of the Psalms, one out of the Prophets, one out of the Gospels, and one out of the writings of Paul. They may be able to read the Bible in a certain amount of time, but most of them wind up like this poor eunuch, reading without understanding. They do not understand the situation described by Paul about the Jews who cannot understand that the law of Moses is really about the Lord Jesus Christ, because they have a veil over their hearts (2 Corinthians 3:13-18).

Many today read the New Testament with the same veil over their hearts. They read it because they have promised to do so and when they do not read, they feel great pangs of guilt. Yet a great many do not really understand.

> 31 *And he said, How can I, except someone should guide me? And he besought Philip to come up and sit with him.*

> 32 *The place of the scripture which he read was this, He was led as a sheep to the slaughter, and like a*

lamb dumb before his shearer, so opened he not his mouth;

33 in his humiliation his judgment was taken away, and who shall declare his generation? for his life is taken from the earth.

34 And the eunuch answered Philip and said, I pray thee, of whom does the prophet speak this? of himself or of some other?

35 Then Philip opened his mouth and began at the same scripture and preached unto him the gospel of Jesus.

36 And as they went on their way, they came unto a certain water; and the eunuch said, See, here is water; what hinders me to be baptized?

The eunuch had studied the Old Testament. He knew that if you were unclean, you had to be washed. When he saw the water, he wanted to take the step with the Lord that he knew about.

37 And Philip said, If thou dost believe with all thine heart, thou may. And he answered and said, I believe that Jesus Christ is the Son of God.

So did Philip respond, "Wait a minute, I have to consult. We have to get Peter and John to come from Jerusalem because I am only the waiter; I am the one that waits on the tables over at the church of Jerusalem. If you want to be baptized in water or in the Holy Spirit, we have to call for an apostle." No, this is not how Philip responded, because he was in direct contact with God.

38 And he commanded the chariot to stand still, and they went both down into the water, both Philip and the eunuch, and he baptized him.

THE MYSTERY OF THE WILL OF GOD

*39 And when they were come up out of the water
the Spirit of the Lord caught away Philip, so that the
eunuch saw him no more, and he went on his way
rejoicing.*

The eunuch went on his way filled with joy, which is a fruit of the Holy Spirit. And the Scriptures do not say that since it was so important to open a work in the land of Ethiopia where the trusted, right-hand person of the queen was now saved, that Philip made arrangements to go or to send someone to begin their indoctrination. No, it says that the Spirit of the Lord caught Philip away once the eunuch was also in direct contact with God. Philip had fulfilled his apostolic mission, and the eunuch saw him no more because the Holy Spirit would continue to guide and comfort the eunuch. Curiously, history bears out that one of the places on earth where there has always been a faithful band of believers is Ethiopia.

> *It is much better to leave the plans and details under the care of the Holy Spirit*

It is much better to leave the plans and details under the care of the Holy Spirit and not think that we must coordinate everything down to the last detail. It is important to explain, teach, and preach under the anointing of the Holy Spirit, but we should not, we must not maintain a people who need to hear from God through us. The person who is truly immersed in the Spirit of God has the possibility of direct communion with God and direct teaching from the Lord. The Holy Spirit can guide us into all truth.

It is also true that the Lord uses his people as a team. He can send Philip first, and then if he chooses, he can send in Peter and John or whatever other person seems best to him.

What happened to Philip?

40 But Philip was found at Azotus, and passing

through, he preached the gospel in all the cities until he came to Caesarea.

Philip was relocated to another place, but Scripture does not give details about how this was accomplished except to say that the Spirit of the Lord caught him away. The rapture that happened to Philip was not to take him out of a place of danger and put him into someplace secure from the problems of this world. He was deposited into another region that had problems and dangers of its own but also where people were open and ready to hear the message. Later in the book of Acts, it mentions a Philip (probably this same person) who had daughters who prophesied.

At the beginning of the book of Acts, the ministry was conducted through men who had come of age, but later on, women were also directly involved. At the beginning, the gospel was just for the Jews, and then it was extended to the Samaritans and also to the Gentiles, the pagans. God opened horizons and borders.

After this episode with Philip, the Lord revealed himself to the very person who was implementing most of the persecution of the Christians, and Saul was converted. However, for the next ten or fifteen years Saul was still called Saul even as he preached and worked for the Lord. But one day some of the Lord's men were praying at a site where the only ministry mentioned was that of prophets and teachers. The Holy Spirit said, *Separate me Barnabas and Saul for the work unto which I have called them.* Several verses later, Saul became Paul (Acts 13:9). God made the change. The name *Paul* means "small or little."

The congregation at Antioch (where the word *Christian* was coined) did not get together and have a meeting to decide how to extend the gospel and evangelize the rest of the world since the Lord had said that the gospel must be preached to all nations. They did not decide to implement the Great Commission with a search for potential missionary candidates. The ministry leaders at Antioch did not decide that they were indispensable to the congregation at Antioch (or that they were the cradle of Christianity) so, therefore, they would make an appeal to the young people and send out missionaries.

No, nothing like that. What actually happened was that they were praying, and the Holy Spirit said, *Separate me Barnabas and Saul for the work unto which I have called them*. God had a plan to evangelize and even ordered the gospel to be presented to the house of Caesar (where, according to Scripture, many were converted). God sent Paul as an ambassador to the house of Caesar, but he did it backwards, not according to our way of thinking. Paul arrived at the palace as a prisoner in chains and ultimately paid with his life, but he left a clean, untainted gospel planted everywhere he went.

Someone said that Paul's greatest mistake was when he did not listen to the prophets who told him what was going to happen to him if he continued back to Jerusalem. A big mistake in Paul's ministry! Well, it depends. From the beginning, God had Ananias tell Paul that he would show him how much it would behoove him to suffer for the cause of Christ, and Paul was willing. He knew what was going to happen to him and went and did it, just as Jesus also knew what would happen and did not shrink back from accomplishing the will of his Father. This is how we got the New Testament! And if Paul had not gone to Jerusalem over the objection of the prophets, we would be missing his prison epistles which have encouraged countless generations of persecuted Christians right up to our present time, when more Christians are being persecuted today than ever before.

Our natural, physical life is not everything, and those who would judge God do not understand this. Those who would accuse God of injustice or even of genocide when he ordered entire nations wiped out in the Old Testament do not understand that there will also be a general resurrection. There will be a fair trial for everyone with an eternal possibility and potential to right every wrong and a promise to wipe away every tear.

Why did God do away with Ananias and Sapphira? Why did God speak in such an abrupt manner with Simon the magician? He was not even given assurance that he would be forgiven. He was told that he was in the gall of bitterness and in the prison of iniquity. He was called to repentance that perhaps he might be forgiven and restored.

We cannot judge God because we have not been behind the veil; we have not yet seen the reality that he is. We have not seen him face to face, much less listened to all that he has to say. The fact that God may do with us as he pleases and that at the same time we are required to be responsible for our actions, must be taken by faith, for the Lord has all eternity to straighten out the effects of the free will that he has bestowed upon us. We are told that everyone will give an account of their actions and for every idle word that came out of their mouths (Matthew 12:36-37). God will leave nothing unresolved, and whoever has suffered injustice will have his day before the throne of God.

There came a time when God had to change the theology of Peter who had been brought up and trained to have nothing to do with Gentiles. But God wanted to send the gospel to the Gentiles, so he showed Peter in many ways that he had to accept the Gentiles as clean, and deal with anyone that God said was clean no matter how wrong this appeared to Peter's natural judgment. God wiped away a huge number of symbols that had become indispensable rites and traditions. God wiped these out when he sent Peter to the house of the Roman centurion while at the same time, he was preparing Saul.

What am I saying? The Lord knows everything. We are not indispensable to explain our rites and rituals to God. He already knows and is much more interested than we are in changing the situation of this world. The real question has always been, "Who is willing to do what God wants, the way God wants it done, and according to the timing of God without trying to protect their own lives and their own interests?" This is what has held us back because many desire to do the work of the Lord their own way and not the Lord's way. The book of the Acts of the Apostles demonstrates God's work being done God's way. This is diametrically opposed to the plans for evangelization invented by man.

Matthew 23

> 15 *Woe unto you, scribes and Pharisees, hypocrites! for ye compass sea and land to make one proselyte, and when he is made, ye make him twofold more a son of hell than yourselves.*

The religion of men trying to indoctrinate adept candidates does not flow by the Spirit or improve people in any way. Instead, according to the Lord, they go from bad to worse.

Where will we be found? Those who were used by the Lord were found faithful with whatever they had at hand. Stephen and Philip were tending tables and waiting on widows. The fact that they became good "waiters" before the Lord cost Stephen his life and launched Philip as an apostle. The Lord is the one who decides how these things turn out. One thing, however, is certain: If we make a decision by the Spirit of God that our own life is not important, and that what is important is the life of the Lord, we can come to the place where we will no longer make decisions based on fear of what others may do to us. We will be guided by the fear of the Lord, which according to Scripture is the beginning of wisdom.

Let us pray:

> *Heavenly Father, we desire to understand, and we desire that what we learn may be fulfilled in actual practice in our lives, that we may be found doing your work and not our own. We ask this in the name of our Lord Jesus Christ. Amen.*

CHAPTER 3

Friends of God

I n chapter 1, we saw the kind of woman that the Lord seeks. We have said that when he finds her, he does not brusquely order her around. He woos her. He draws her. He invites her. There is a level upon which the Lord gives orders to slaves and servants, but in the realm of friendship, courtship, and marriage, this is not what he does. It is a dull and dreary marriage when the husband only gives orders to the wife. Many married couples live in misery because their hearts are no longer in love. Jesus does not want to marry a slave or a servant. The relationship between the Lord and his true bride is compared in Scripture to a courtship that culminates in a wedding.

Therefore, there is a relationship far beyond that of a slave or of a servant with the master. This is clear in the gospel:

John 15

14 *Ye are my friends if ye do whatsoever I command you.*

15 *From now on I do not call you slaves, for the slave does not know what his lord does; but I have called you friends, for all things that I have heard of my Father I have made known unto you.*

*16 Ye have not chosen me, but I have chosen you
and ordained you, that ye should go and bring forth
fruit, and that your fruit should remain; that whatsoever ye shall ask of the Father in my name, he may
give it unto you.*

17 This I command you, that ye love one another.

*18 If the world hates you, ye know that it hated me
before it hated you.*

We must be very careful not to confuse the different pictures
that are described in Scripture, because the Lord will show us
things from many different angles. In one picture he is the
groom, and we are his promised bride; one day there will be a
great wedding ceremony. In another picture he is the head, and
we are the body of Christ. In another picture he is the vine, and
we are the branches. In yet another he is the rock, and we are
the temple that he is building of living stones. Upon this rock is
the foundation of his congregation. We cannot take these pictures out of context and begin to adorn them according to our
own whims. They must come together as the Lord has placed
them in Scripture in the light of the Holy Spirit.

Song of Solomon 2

*1 I am the lily of the field {Heb. Sharon} and the rose
of the valleys.*

*2 As the lily among thorns, so is my love among the
virgins.*

We are now in the stage of the lily. This is the second stage
– the stage of entering into the new covenant. The lily is a symbol of the priesthood of all believers. Jesus is the great High
Priest, and when we are born again and baptized into the Holy
Spirit, we can blossom as the lily. The wisdom available to us by

the Holy Spirit is greater than the wisdom that Solomon had because the Holy Spirit flows through us (Matthew 6:28-29; Luke 12:27). Anyone filled with the Holy Spirit has access to all the wisdom of God. The Lord can flow in and through this person according to his will as long as the person is concerned with cleanliness and purity.

There is, however, one drawback regarding the lily. It is temporal. The gifts and ministries of the Spirit are only for a time and a season. For the Lord is not content to just have a garden full of beautiful flowers. He desires fruit – fruit that has come to maturity – so he may feed those he cares about. He desires to plant and reproduce more of the same (remember, the seed is in the fruit). The flower of the lily is beautiful, but it is not a seed and will not relieve hunger. If the Lord has given us gifts or talents, there is no guarantee that we will always have these tomorrow. The guarantee is that if we are faithful with gifts and talents today, in the future we will be given more. We will be given things that endure (1 Corinthians 13).

The guarantee is that if we are faithful with gifts and talents today, in the future we will be given more.

So we are given gifts, we are given talents, we are given the capacity to bloom as the lily for a fleeting moment in time while the natural life that we have transpires. But at the moment of our death, or when the Lord returns, we will be required to give an account of what we have done with gifts, ministries, and talents. This is why there was an *open flower* of pure gold engraved on the crown or mitre of the high priest according to the law of Moses. The inscription on this crown read, *HOLINESS UNTO THE LORD* (Exodus 28:36-39).

The flower is nothing unless it receives a little grain of pollen so that the flower can produce the seed. If we have not received the incorruptible seed of *HOLINESS UNTO THE*

LORD, something terrible could happen, and we could reproduce a cross strain of spiritual bastards that will be disqualified
from the inheritance. The realm of the flower, of the lily, of our
present gifts and talents is but the earnest or down payment. It
is not the fullness of our inheritance (2 Corinthians 1:22; 5:5;
Ephesians 1:14).

The living word of God {Gr. ho logos} will form a bride that
is without spot or wrinkle or any such thing who will be able to
represent the Lord as he is. This lady will be responsible with
all the authority that pertains to her husband. We will see this
develop and come forth as the Lord brings her into maturity.
Notice her early perception of her lover:

> 3 *As the apple tree among the trees of the wild, so*
> *is my beloved among the sons. I desired to sit under*
> *his shadow, and his fruit was sweet to my taste.*

This is yet another confirmation that the covering is not
delegated human ministry. He is the covering. She desires to
be under his covering and to be nourished by fruit produced
directly by him. Our problem started under an apple tree when
Eve listened to the wrong voice and took and ate the wrong
apple. Now our restoration must be effected under a different
apple tree desiring his covering and feeding on what he says, not
listening to other voices or spirits. Look at what happens next!

> 4 *He brought me to the wine chamber and placed*
> *his banner of love over me.*

His covering is getting more and more interesting. His banner is his flag or standard. Wine is a symbol of life. He joins
her to his life, and this life is found under his covering, under
his banner, which becomes a more and more "narrow way." He
identifies her with everything he stands for. His flag or standard
indicates his manner of doing things. His love is different from
other kinds of love. Man's love is one thing. God's love is quite

another. God's love is born of sacrifice and redeems by its very nature. Man's love is self-seeking, always looking for something in return. God's love is not like that at all.

He is bringing her into a love that only he has and that only comes from him. It is necessary for his love to totally dominate her being until she no longer reacts to circumstances according to the dictates of man's love or as a reaction to the lack of man's love. There will be tests and trials, and she will discover some startling things regarding her own heart. He will manage all this without giving her orders, but rather only invitations in the bond that he has with her through his love. Soon she realizes that without his love she can no longer live.

> 5 *Sustain me with flagons of wine, strengthen me*
> *with apples; for I am sick with love.*

She knows that what she is receiving from him cannot be obtained anywhere else or with anyone else. This is so unique, so sublime, so different from anything else that she has ever known.

> 6 *His left hand is under my head, and his right hand*
> *embraces me.*

Then comes the phrase *I charge you* that is repeated three more times in this short book for a total of four times. When something is repeated twice in Scripture, it is very important. When it is stated three times, God is setting something in place that he does not want changed. When he puts it in four times, it is a divine statute, something that is according to his nature. Four is a heavenly number. The sun, moon, and stars, the great lights, and the heavenly hosts were created on the fourth day. Four is a number that represents the love of God that is heavenly, not earthly. He is now engraving a very strong statement upon her heart:

*7 I charge you, O ye virgins of Jerusalem, by the roes
and by the hinds of the field that ye not awake nor
stir up love, until he pleases.*

This has application in both the natural and the spiritual realms. If the deep, profound sentiments of our heart are awakened or stirred up at the wrong time, with the wrong person, a bond will be formed in the soul that can be extremely difficult to break. Look what happened when Dinah, Jacob's daughter, bonded with the son of Hamor the Hivite of Shechem (Genesis 34).

How many young ladies have been scarred for life because they opened that most intimate place in their heart to the wrong man? In the natural, the Lord is saying to wait until he approves the relationship. This is true with any intimate friendship or relationship.

In the spiritual realm, he is saying that there is an intimate place in our being that corresponds to the Holy of Holies (for we are the temple). If we embrace the wrong spirit and let a spirit that is not the Holy Spirit into our Holy of Holies, there will be a terrible abomination. How do unclean religious spirits captivate so many people? How is it that a person can enter a religion so easily, but no one can get them out of it?

It is because their souls have bonded with a spirit that is not the Holy Spirit. They are now joined to something that they think is God or that they think comes from God, but it is not so. It is much harder to deliver a religious person from this type of error than a prostitute who knows what she is doing is sin. This is why Jesus said the sinners and publicans were closer to the kingdom of God than the scribes and Pharisees (Matthew 21:28-32).

In order for the Devil to flee from us, we must resist him. In order to resist him, we must first leave our pride and arrogance behind and submit to the mighty hand of God (James

4:6-7). The person who intimately embraces a wrong religious spirit will soon be filled with arrogance and pride, thinking that somehow they are spiritually superior to everyone else. After embracing a false spirit, they are incapable of resisting a demon even when they have him inside, because now they think that their demon is an angel of light.

The warning to *not awake nor stir up love, until he pleases* is given three times.

Paul said that his ministry was to present believers as chaste virgins to Christ, as candidates for marriage (2 Corinthians 11:2). Our past is not important because God wipes away our past when we are born again. No matter how filthy or despicable our past, the Lord Jesus can wipe it all away. God is not interested in rehabilitating or restoring our old man with its old nature. God wants to kill it and bring us forth as a new creation in Christ. And when we come forth as a new creation, he does not want us contaminated with a spirit that is not holy.

> *Our past is not important because God wipes away our past when we are born again.*

After we are born again, if we seek baptism in a spirit that is not holy, because we see many apparent miracles and supernatural events but do not check that the real fruit of the Holy Spirit is being produced, and the Lord has indeed ordained for us to be involved and to open up the most intimate place in our heart, we could be overrun by the enemy; our last state could end up worse than our first state (Hebrews 4). If we are a *chaste virgin*, we will not be engaged in any spiritual promiscuity.

People flock to the church where everyone is falling over backwards when the pastor waves his cape or the next religious spectacle is being presented. They move the people out of guilt instead of allowing real conviction of the Holy Spirit. With the human ministry of twisting arms, manipulating, and fleecing, all manner of unclean spirits present themselves as angels of light. Those who respond to these appeals and offer their lives on an unclean altar seeking to use the things of God for personal gain and obtain the things of this world, will bond with ministry that is not clean and disqualify themselves from a marriage with the Lord.

The Lord desires a clean bride without spot or wrinkle and a clean marriage. This can only happen to us if we watch over our most intimate parts and do not *awake or stir up love, until he pleases*. This is one of the most serious warnings in Scripture and one of the first things that the Holy Spirit will begin to write on the tablets of the heart and mind of anyone who is a candidate for being part of the true bride of Christ under the new covenant.

We may have slightly unqualified friends in the outer court of our being and even closer inside in the holy place of our lives (which is a place of preparation), but the Holy of Holies of our being is a place reserved only for the Lord (and for those whom the Lord explicitly approves of because he has cleansed them and approved of our relationship with them). We are the temple of God. If we do not take this seriously, we will be deceived. Eve's downfall was not just when she took the bite out of the apple. It began when she opened up her being to the wrong voice. Then Adam listened to Eve instead of to the Lord, and everything came down around them.

The only one who will not be deceived in these matters is the Lord, and this is why we must depend directly on him. If our motive is to find any other satisfaction in life than to please the Lord, we will fall short of the high calling (Philippians 3:14). The woman in the Song of Solomon is seeing this clearer and clearer. Notice where she is placing her priorities:

> 8 *The voice of my beloved! behold, he comes leaping over the mountains, skipping over the hills.*

9 *My beloved is like a roe or a young hart; behold, he stands behind our wall; he looks through the windows, blossoming through the lattice.*

She desires to hear his voice more than anything else. She is tuned to his voice and to everything about him. Hearing his voice has a cleansing effect on her heart, and this is opening her eyes. Her revelation is not yet perfect, for she sees him *blossoming through the lattice.* Paul says that *now we see as through a mirror, in darkness,* but the time will come when we shall see him face to face (1 Corinthians 13:12).

She is happy at the banquet of the feast of Pentecost; she is thrilled with the stage of the lily; she is enthused with her gifts and talents; she basks in his love and in his life in the wine chamber; she is hearing his voice, and every now and then she even gets a glimpse of him through the lattice. But now comes a serious invitation:

10 *My beloved spoke and said unto me, Rise up, my love, my fair one, and come away.*

This is an invitation, not a threat.

11 *For, behold, the winter is past; the rain is over and gone;*

12 *the flowers appear on the earth; the time of the song is come, and the voice of the turtle dove has been heard in our land;*

13 *the fig tree has put forth her green figs, and the vines in blossom have given forth their fragrance. Arise, my love, my fair one, and come away.*

He is calling for her to leave the comfort of the banquet and follow him wherever he goes. She does not know what will happen; she only knows he is calling for her to come with him.

She knows that he is like a roe or a young hart, and he can leap over any obstacle. Nothing can stop him. But the very thought of attempting to bound away with him worries her. She feels very secure at the banquet.

There are many who love to be somewhere listening to an anointed word with great communion with other saints where they feel the life and love of the Lord. But this is only to build us up so that we can come away with him as he gives a specific call to each one that he has chosen.

He may want us to go and visit some prisoners, or help a prostitute, or go somewhere uncomfortable to a faraway city or wilderness and encourage those who live there. The call to each one will be very different. And if you tell the Lord that you are willing to do whatever he desires except this, that, or the other thing, guess where he is going to test and prove you? If you desire to qualify as the bride of Christ, it is best not to place any conditions.

If you desire to qualify as the bride of Christ, it is best not to place any conditions.

14 *O my dove, that art in the clefts of the rock, in the secret places of the stairs, let me see thy counte-nance, let me hear thy voice; for sweet is thy voice, and thy countenance is beautiful.*

So she hides in the wine cellar. He does not condemn her. He encourages her with his voice. He coaxes her to come out of hiding and show her face. He tells us that we have not because we ask not, and many times when we ask, we ask amiss. He wants to hear her say, "Do in me according to thy will ... thy kingdom come, thy will be done." She still has a lot of fear, and she says something very profound that saves the day, and she is not disqualified.

15 *Hunt the foxes for us, the little foxes, that spoil*
the vines; for our vines are in blossom.

What are those foxes? Could it be that those little, beautiful, playful foxes are causing problems? If they play with the
vines and bite the flowers, the flowers are damaged. There will
be no fruit: *Ye shall know them by their fruit.* They represent
the little, seemingly innocent things in our lives that rob us of
victory. She is there, hiding in the cleft of the rock by the stairs
of the wine cellar, and she knows that unless these little foxes
are brought under control, there may be no more wine.

These little, darling foxes have the ability to disqualify us
and keep us from ever becoming fruitful. She still doubts that
she can keep up with him if she leaves her place of apparent
safety, but she says, "Hunt the foxes for me. Lord, track down
and kill anything in me that would prevent me from becoming
fruitful in your kingdom. I don't care how pretty or wonderful
these things seem on the surface. I dare not be disqualified.
Please make me fruitful."

Now she makes another statement, which she will modify
two more times before she finally gets it right.

16 *My beloved is mine, and I am his; he feeds among*
the lilies.

She is possessive of him and will not give up, and yes, she
also realizes that she belongs to him.

17 *Until the day breaks and the shadows flee away,*
return, my beloved, and be thou like a roe or a
young hart upon the mountains of Bether.

Bether means "separation" and symbolizes our need to have
whatever causes harm separated out of us. Notice that she did
not go away with him even though she realizes that he will
only feed among the lilies until the day breaks. He left and she

did not come out of the cleft in the rock by the secret place of the stairs. She does not realize what will happen because she rejected his invitation. Her saving grace is that she did authorize him to hunt down the little foxes.

And so it is with most of us. We fear coming out of our comfort zones, turning our back on the things of this world, and burning our bridges behind us to leave with him. Embarking on this adventure with him over those mountains and into those dangerous places seems like too much of a risk. We know that he can do all these things, but we doubt that we can do it even after he has clearly called us. She was secure in her little refuge and look what happened:

Song of Solomon 3

1 *By night on my bed I sought him whom my soul loves; I sought him, but I did not find him.*

Now it dawns on her that it was not the wine chamber itself that had given her such a sense of security. She was secure because she had not been alone; he had been there with her. Her refuge in the cleft of the rock had only worked while he was nearby. When he left and she did not follow him, she remained alone. Now it is always night for her because night is where he is not.

2 *I will rise now and go about the city in the streets, and in the broad ways I will seek him whom my soul loves; I sought him, but I did not find him.*

In great desperation, she is leaving her spot of apparent security. She searches frantically and is unable to locate him. We tend to think that when he says, "Follow me," and we do not go with him, that later we can do so whenever we please, and he will still be patiently waiting for us. This is not necessarily the case. When he gives the invitation, Scripture says, *Today if ye will hear his voice.* We may not be able to hear tomorrow if we do not respond today. She continues her desperate search and is unable to find him. She realizes now that she has committed a terrible mistake.

> 3 *The watchmen that go about the city found me, to*
> *whom I said, Have ye seen him whom my soul loves?*

It appears that they had not. God has placed watchmen, but the watchmen cannot connect us directly with the Lord. They can warn us when we are alone and tell us that it is dangerous to wander alone at night in the city, but they cannot automatically put us back into union with the Lord.

> 4 *It was but a little that I passed from them that*
> *I found him whom my soul loves: I held him and*
> *would not let him go until I had brought him into*
> *my mother's house and into the chamber of her that*
> *brought me into the light.*

She was still not very willing to go with him wherever he chose, but she insisted on bringing him back into her *mother's house.* We want to lock in the anointing of the presence of the Lord at our group, our church, or the place where we were born spiritually. This is another stage of immaturity. The law of liberty is different. If he is doing other things and goes somewhere else, that is his business. If he does not show up at our meeting, then why should we?

> 5 *I charge you, O ye virgins of Jerusalem, by the roes*
> *and by the hinds of the field, that ye not awake nor*
> *stir up love, until he pleases.*

She repeats the warning at her mother's place. She understands more and more about not opening up the intimate areas of our heart to anyone or anything not expressly authorized by him. We must wait for him to take the initiative in this most vital area. We must not open this door to anyone but him. She is acquiring wisdom about how to handle the virgins of Jerusalem and even her own mother. This, along with her authorization to let him hunt down the foxes, will assure her that his courtship of her will continue.

> 6 *Who is she that rises out of the wilderness like pillars of smoke, perfumed with myrrh and frankincense and with all the aromatic powders?*

The children of Israel had their formation in the desert where they were readied for their inheritance in the Promised Land. This wilderness is a type of the church age as the bride of Christ comes to maturity (same word in Hebrew and Greek as *perfection*). When Israel was about to cross the Jordan River into the Promised Land, Scripture says the fear of them fell on all the inhabitants of Jericho.

This woman is also a symbol of a clean congregation that the Lord is preparing as his bride. The day is fast approaching when we will enter into the fullness of our inheritance in Christ. This is the day of the Lord. She is perfumed with myrrh (the way of the cross) and frankincense (the love of God flowing through her) and with all the aromatic powders (the character of God evident in her). She is beginning to attract attention and strike fear into the hearts of all the enemies of the people of God.

> 7 *Behold it is the bed of Solomon; sixty valiant men are about it of the valiant of Israel.*

> 8 *They all hold swords, being expert in war; each one has his sword upon his thigh because of the fears of the night.*

> 9 *King Solomon made himself a palanquin of the wood of Lebanon.*

10 He made its pillars of silver, the bottom of it of gold, the covering of it of purple, its interior being paved with love, for the virgins of Jerusalem.

11 Go forth, O ye virgins of Zion, and behold King Solomon with the crown with which his mother crowned him in the day of his espousals, and in the day of the gladness of his heart.

She is now the vehicle to carry the anointing and the glory of God. She is the example for all the virgins of Jerusalem. The protection of the king surrounds her (for he shall give his angels charge over you). Not one hair of her head can be touched without his permission. King Solomon made this palanquin, or vehicle, of pillars of silver (redemption), a bottom of gold (the steps of the righteous are ordered by the Lord), and a covering of purple (she is royalty).

> *Not one hair of her head can be touched without his permission.*

She has learned how to relate to her earthly mother (the congregation among which she was born into the light) and is now a shining example to the virgins of Jerusalem. As the heavens are beginning to open unto her, she begins to perceive his mother, the Jerusalem from above, which is the mother of us all (Galatians 4:26), when we are in Christ.

Stephen saw the heavens opened unto him on the day that he was martyred. The apostle Paul was taken up into the third heaven and shown things that were not lawful for him to reveal here on earth. Isaiah saw the king in all his glory and was almost undone. The "chaste virgins" of all of history have had revelations of this glory. They understand how the final battle is to be won. Millions of witnesses (Greek *martyrs*) have gone forth as he has sent them.

Revelation 12

11 *And they have overcome him by the blood of the Lamb and by the word of their testimony; and they loved not their lives unto the death..*

Ephesians 2

19 *Now therefore ye are no longer strangers and for-eigners, but fellowcitizens with the saints and of the household of God,*

20 *and are built upon the foundation of the apostles and prophets, Jesus Christ himself being the chief cornerstone.*

Let us pray:

Heavenly Father, please help us hunt down the little foxes that would prevent us from bearing good fruit. Bring us to fruitfulness. May you delight in us. We ask this in the name of our Lord Jesus. Amen.

CHAPTER 4

The Path to Maturity

The persecution of the Christians at Jerusalem by the religious authorities had many consequences. The apostles had stayed in Jerusalem, and everyone else fled to Judea, Samaria, and elsewhere. Scripture says that the congregations (churches) were multiplied. It is important to understand that the word *congregation* {Gr. ekklesia or called out ones} translated "church" in many English Bibles is used in plural in many Scriptures. The book of Acts does not speak of a single congregation or church; it speaks of many congregations and of the congregations or churches being multiplied.

This is not referring to an institution. This word *ekklesia* means "those who are called out" of the institution, those who have come out of organized religion. They met in homes for the first two centuries. The word always identifies people or a congregation but never a building or institution. It is not perfectly in line with Scripture to refer to an "early church" or to a "first-century church," for there were many churches or congregations. In fact, our English word *church* is most unfortunate in that it is of dubious pagan origin. This is why the *Jubilee Bible* translation uses the word *congregation* in italics with a footnote {Gr. ekklesia – called out ones}.

The Scripture is clear that there is but one body of Christ

of which the Lord Jesus is the Head. He is the only Mediator of the new covenant. He is the government of the many members of the body of Christ. There is only one body of Christ, but there are many congregations (churches) in the book of Acts (Acts 9:31; 16:5).

Look at how man, over the centuries, has twisted things by saying there is only one universal church and many local bodies. This is not true. If there are local bodies of Christ, then someone may claim to be the local head of the local body. The Lord Jesus is the Head, and there is only one body

> *If there are local bodies of Christ, then someone may claim to be the local head of the local body.*

(Ephesians 4:4). There are not many bodies of Christ; there are many congregations (mistranslated long ago as "churches"). There are many groups of people called by God to leave the system of this world, the system of men, and the system of religion organized by man. They may be as small as two or three individuals (Matthew 18:20).

Matthew 13:24-30 describes the tares being sown by the enemy in the same field as the wheat, and being allowed by the master of the house to remain in the field (which represents the kingdom of the heavens). At the time of the harvest, they are bundled and burned before the wheat is harvested.

In Acts chapter 9, there are important details that are not apparent at first. The Lord Jesus revealed himself to Saul, and Saul was the one who was persecuting the true congregation (church). He was dragging men and women off to prison. He had participated in the death of Stephen. But when Saul arrived in Damascus, he was blind. Someone had to lead him by the hand. After a direct encounter with the Lord Jesus, he could not see anyone.

Jesus had told him to *Arise and go into the city, and it shall be told thee what it behooves thee to do.* Saul was so shaken by this that he did nothing but wait for instructions. For three days, he neither ate nor drank while he waited. During this time, the Lord spoke in a vision to a disciple named Ananias and told him to go and minister to Saul. Ananias had his doubts; he told the Lord about all the evil that Saul had been doing and how great a threat Saul was. But the Lord told Ananias to go anyway. Ananias did not have to go and consult with some elders or clergy in order to get permission to minister unto Saul. No, Ananias went, risking his life; but he was secure in the word that he had received directly from the Lord. If Ananias was mistaken in what he heard from the Lord, he could be in real trouble because Saul had come to Damascus for the express purpose of harming the believers.

Saul was also risking his life because after the Lord spoke to him, he desisted from doing anything on his own until he had a word from the Lord. Saul did not even drink any water. How long can people last in the desert without water? Three days is probably close to the limit. This was a test of faith for Ananias, but it was also a test of faith for Saul.

In the book of the Acts of the Apostles, the word *disciple* is used frequently. This word begins in the Gospels where the disciple is the one who leaves everything to follow the Lord. He does not count on having anything of his own; everything is in the hands of the Lord. The Lord does not treat every disciple exactly the same. In Acts 8, Philip went to Samaria where there were many signs, wonders, and miracles taking place. Many believed but no one received the Holy Spirit. The Holy Spirit was imparted when the apostles came from Jerusalem and laid their hands on the believers. (And someone even offered them money for this power.)

In the case of the conversion of Saul, Saul had a direct encounter with the Lord Jesus, and the Lord sent a disciple, not an apostle, to minister to Saul three days later. But here is something very interesting:

Acts 9

17 *Then Ananias went and entered into the house; and putting his hands on him said, Brother Saul, the Lord Jesus who appeared unto thee in the way as thou didst come, has sent me, that thou might receive thy sight and be filled with the Holy Spirit.*

18 *And immediately there fell from his eyes as it had been scales; and he received sight immediately and arose and was baptized.*

19 *And when he had received food, he was comforted.*

This word *comforted* is a word that is linked with the action of the Holy Spirit because he is the Comforter.

How is it that the Holy Spirit was only imparted to the Samaritans by the laying on of hands by the apostles Peter and John? One chapter later a disciple is sent, and Saul receives the Holy Spirit. How about this? The book of Acts is full of examples. Philip was supposedly a waiter, not a preacher. He had been appointed as a deacon (servant) when all of a sudden he wound up preaching in Samaria with signs and wonders following until he was caught up and transported by the Spirit!

What is the difference between a disciple and an apostle? In the Gospels the Lord called his disciples. To be a disciple at least two things had to happen: (1) The Lord had to call them, and (2) they had to leave everything and follow him. But when the disciples became apostles, it was simple: the Lord sent them out to represent himself. After they came back, having done what the Lord sent them to do, the Scripture simply says, *Now the names of the twelve apostles are these...* Nowhere in the Gospels is there a ceremony where apostles are appointed. Interesting!

Here was the disciple Ananias, and the Lord sent him to do what only an apostle could do, and everything went perfectly. Don't you think it is interesting that the Lord can send whomever he wants to do whatever he ordains whenever he chooses?

The Lord Jesus Christ is the first of the firstfruits, the beginning of the new creation. And we can enter into the new creation in him, in his life.

John 3

> 34 *For he whom God has sent speaks the words of God; for God does not give the Spirit by measure unto him.*

What does this mean?

The person who is sent by God to do the will of God will receive an unlimited anointing to fulfill whatever is in the heart of God for him or her to accomplish! This is not an anointing by measure such as the carefully prepared formula described in Exodus chapter 30 that was to be poured over every prophet, priest, and king in Israel. (I am told that the exact formula yields two gallons of anointing oil.) This is not the anointing of Pentecost that provided gifts of the Spirit or even a double portion such as received by Elisha.

This is the anointing described in Psalm 133. This is the anointing that Jesus had from his Father. He only came to speak the words of the Father and do the deeds of the Father. We are able to perceive glimpses of this in the book of the Acts of the Apostles, but the fullness is reserved for the time of the end (Revelation 10 and 11).

The problem we have today is that many who claim to be Christians are not even disciples. In the book of Acts, in God's terminology, there is no alternate word. Those who follow the

Lord Jesus are called disciples, and if they follow the Lord, they cannot be following their own whims and desires. (Simon the magician found out about that!)

This does not mean that the person must leave what they have been doing. Late in the book of Acts, after the apostle Paul had been sent by God and it was confirmed that God had designated him as the apostle to the Gentiles with wonderful results in many places, the apostle kept doing what he had always done: he made tents and sold them to meet his expenses (Acts 18:2-3). In this way, he could present the gospel without cost to the Corinthians and others. He chose to work with his hands and not ask for money, so he continued with his tentmaking profession. Is this not pertinent?

A call to follow the Lord, even being sent out by the Lord as an apostle, is not necessarily a call to stop working with your hands and operate only within the spiritual realm. Nor is there an example in the book of Acts of anyone seeking higher education with rabbis or of anyone wanting to be a rabbi. To be a disciple means that Jesus is directly in charge, and the disciple is willing to be like Ananias. If the Lord tells a disciple to risk his life, his life is not his own; it belongs to the Lord. And if the Lord sends us on a mission such as the apostolic mission he assigned to Ananias, we will flow in the apostolic realm.

In the book of Acts, there was a meeting among the apostles and believers to select people for ministry, but this meeting was to pick seven waiters to serve at the tables of widows who were being helped by the congregation. They chose waiters so the apostles could be available for spiritual ministry with the Word of God. They all came together and made sure that the seven men had evidence of the fruit of the Spirit and were qualified to serve at the dinner tables.

But the first two waiters on the list soon accelerated into incredible ministries. Stephen confounded the Jews, preaching with power and authority which was backed up by signs and wonders. When the Jews were unable to answer him, they killed him. This was similar to what happened with Jesus.

The Spirit also moved Philip in ministry when the apostles and congregation thought they had assigned him to wait on tables. Philip, who was designated a waiter, wound up sparking a huge revival in Samaria, baptizing a high-level official from a kingdom in Africa, imparting the Holy Spirit,

> *Philip, who was designated a waiter, wound up sparking a huge revival in Samaria*

and being caught up and transported by the Spirit into an additional realm of ministry as well as raising up daughters who prophesied.

Philip did not back off and attempt to consult with the apostles when God began to move him. He did not ask permission from men to do what the angel of the Lord ordered him to do. Neither did Ananias. Ananias did not say to the Lord, "But the Holy Spirit is only imparted when the apostles lay their hands on the believer, and the apostles are in Jerusalem. Should I go and get them?" No, Ananias believed the Lord and went by faith and did the work of an apostle.

Acts 10

1 *There was a certain man in Caesarea called Cornelius, a centurion of the company called the Italian,*

Cornelius was a Roman centurion commanding Roman troops. This is noteworthy because there could have been companies of soldiers from other nations who would not have had the power or prestige of the Romans.

2 *a devout man and one that feared God with all his house, who gave many alms to the people and prayed to God always.*

Alms to the people in this context means acts of mercy. The word *alms* comes from the word *mercy*. It is the same as when the Lord Jesus went out and along the way saw people who were in need. Scripture says that he had mercy or compassion on them so he healed them. Sometimes he also told them they were saved, and their sins were forgiven. He told them he did nothing on his own but only spoke what the Father was saying and did what the Father was doing. Interesting! The Lord Jesus felt compassion, did the miracle, and then said that he was not doing anything that his Father was not doing.

Cornelius was doing acts of compassion; he was a person who feared God, and Scripture says he was a devout man (devout means "like God").

> 3 *He saw in a vision evidently about the ninth hour*
> *of the day an angel of God coming in to him and*
> *saying unto him, Cornelius.*

The part about the ninth hour is interesting because in the gospel of Luke in the first chapter, a priest named Zacharias has his turn to tend the altar of incense, which was located in the Holy of Holies but was tended from the Holy Place. While he was doing this, people were outside praying. Later in the New Testament it says that the prayer time in the temple was the ninth hour. It appears that they counted the hours from dawn, so the ninth hour would be about 3:00 p.m. This was their prayer time. It was at the ninth hour when Peter and John raised up the paralytic and gave a message to the multitude congregated there for prayer. They were arrested and gave the rest of their message later to the Sanhedrin after being put on trial.

Many things in the Gospels and in the book of Acts occur at the ninth hour just as many things in Jesus' ministry take place on the seventh day (the Sabbath). And this caused much controversy.

So Cornelius was in his house doing what the Jews were doing at the temple at the ninth hour. And the plan of God was that his temple would be the people who surrender to him. (One thing that most people forget is that prayer is not just us making petitions to God; prayer is also God's response to us.) Cornelius had not yet received the Holy Spirit, but God sent him an angel. Just as God sent an angel to Zacharias and to Mary, he sent an angel to Cornelius, the Roman centurion.

What did the angel say to Cornelius? Was the message, "Careful Cornelius. It is extremely serious that you are part of an imperialist army with such a bad record. The Roman army is oppressing the entire world and treading the people of God underfoot. Cornelius, you need to repent; resign from this wicked army at once!"

Is this what the angel said? No. He called him by name, and this is what happened:

> 4 *And when he had looked on him, he was afraid*
> *and said, What is it, Lord? And he said unto him,*
> *Thy prayers and thine alms* {lit. thine acts of mercy}
> *are come up for a memorial before God.*

God gave Cornelius an answer similar to the answer given to Daniel when God heard his prayer (Daniel 10:12).

> 5 *And now send men to Joppa and call for one*
> *Simon, whose surname is Peter;*

> 6 *he lodges with one Simon a tanner, whose house*
> *is by the sea side; he shall tell thee what it behooves*
> *thee to do.*

Does this not seem strange? An angel of God came from the presence of God directly to Cornelius, the centurion, and instead of giving a direct revelation, he commanded him to send for Peter in order to know what God really wanted.

God spoke well of John the Baptist. He said that among those born of women, none were greater than John the Baptist, but that the least in the kingdom of heaven was greater than he.

Scripture says that the angels are watching us with great interest to see what God does with us (1 Peter 1:12). Scripture also says that those who are born again and have the Spirit of God will become greater than the angels.

The Lord sent an angel and the presence of the angel frightened Cornelius, who did not know what to do. The angel gave little explanation and did not hold forth a lot of wise counsel. He only let Cornelius know that something about him had caught the attention of God who had sent an angel with instructions, and the instructions were that he was to call for Peter.

The Lord Jesus Christ is the Son of God, and God's plan is for Jesus to have many brethren.

What God has placed into the hands of human beings who have repented, are converted, born again, and full of the presence of the Holy Spirit is greater than what is taking place with the angels. Scripture says that God has never called one of the angels his Son (Hebrews 1:4-8). The Lord Jesus Christ is the Son of God, and God's plan is for Jesus to have many brethren.

> 7 *And when the angel who spoke unto Cornelius was departed, he called two of his household servants and a devout soldier of those that waited on him continually;*
>
> 8 *and when he had declared all these things unto them, he sent them to Joppa.*
>
> 9 *On the morrow, as they went on their journey and drew near unto the city, Peter went up upon the housetop to pray about the sixth hour;*

This was about noon, and Peter was going to pray about three hours before the prayer time of the Jews.

10 and he became very hungry and would have eaten; but while they made ready, he fell into a rapture of understanding

11 and saw the heaven opened and a certain vessel descending unto him, as it had been a great sheet knit at the four corners and let down to the earth,

12 in which were all manner of fourfooted beasts of the earth and wild beasts and reptiles and fowls of the air.

13 And there came a voice to him, Rise, Peter, kill and eat.

14 But Peter said, Not so, Lord; for I have never eaten anything that is common or unclean.

15 And the voice spoke unto him the second time, That which God has cleansed, do not call common.

16 This was done three times, and the vessel was received up again into heaven.

17 Now while Peter doubted in himself what this vision which he had seen should mean, behold, the men who were sent from Cornelius had made enquiry for Simon's house and stood before the gate

18 and called and asked whether Simon, who was surnamed Peter, were lodged there.

19 While Peter thought on the vision, the Spirit said unto him, Behold, three men seek thee.

20 *Arise therefore and get thee down and go with them, doubting nothing; for I have sent them.*

The Holy Spirit had clear communication with Peter. The communication with Ananias had also been clear. The revelation of the Lord Jesus to Saul was done in such a way that there could be no misunderstanding.

Today many claim to be led by God and claim that God has spoken to them, yet they continue to have a lot of confusion. Once I complained about not hearing the voice of the Lord with clarity. However, a few weeks later I was kidnapped, and after a few days of being tied to a tree out in the jungle, I started to hear the voice of God with much greater clarity. I was able to hear much better!

Desiring things that are not the will of God tends to drown out the still, small voice of the Lord. Those who are hearing the voice of God in the book of Acts are the disciples who had made the decision to follow the Lord without looking back. They had counted the cost, and they knew that the price could be their own lives. When things are defined like this, it is much easier to hear the voice of God. Even Saul, when Scripture says he was still breathing out threats and slaughtering the disciples of the Lord, thought he was leaving all his personal ambitions behind in order to rid the land of Israel of the heretics of this Way. The Lord spoke to him in a very clear manner, not just with his voice (Saul's companions heard the voice), but also with his presence that left him blind.

19 *While Peter thought on the vision,*

Notice this: He had seen something, he had also heard something, and the Holy Spirit continued to speak to him; this was continual communion.

21 *Then Peter went down to the men who were sent unto him from Cornelius and said, Behold, I am*

he whom ye seek; what is the cause for which ye are come?

22 *And they said, Cornelius the centurion, a just man and one that fears God and of good report among all the nation of the Jews, was warned from God by a holy angel to send for thee into his house and to hear words of thee.*

23 *Then he called them in and lodged them. And on the morrow Peter went away with them, and certain brethren from Joppa accompanied him.*

24 *And the next day they entered into Caesarea. And Cornelius waited for them and had called together his kinsmen and near friends.*

25 *And as Peter was coming in, Cornelius met him and fell down at his feet and worshipped him.*

26 *But Peter took him up, saying, Stand up; I myself also am a man.*

27 *And as he talked with him, he went in and found many that were come together.*

28 *And he said unto them, Ye know how that it is an abominable thing for a man that is a Jew to keep company or come unto one of another nation; but God has showed me that I should not call any man common or unclean.*

29 *Therefore I came unto you without doubting, as soon as I was sent for; I ask therefore for what intent ye have sent for me?*

30 *And Cornelius said, Four days ago I was fasting*

until this hour; and at the ninth hour I prayed in my house, and, behold, a man stood before me in bright clothing

31 *and said, Cornelius, thy prayer is heard and thine alms are had in remembrance in the sight of God.*

We know that our own good works that we come up with cannot save us; but a person who is moved by the heart of God to do the will of God is in a very different situation. The work that God does in our heart and the work that God does through us after changing our heart is acceptable to God.

32 *Send therefore to Joppa, and call here Simon, whose surname is Peter; he is lodged in the house of one Simon a tanner by the sea side, who, when he comes, shall speak unto thee.*

33 *Immediately therefore I sent to thee, and thou hast done well to come. Now therefore we are all here present before God to hear all things that are commanded thee of God.*

According to the Jews, the presence of God was in Jerusalem in the Holy of Holies. Cornelius had the revelation that God was in Caesarea, in his house, with his family. They were in the presence of God. This was a great revelation and nothing like this is previously recorded in Scripture.

Cornelius knew he was in the presence of God. Why? Because God no longer lives in temples made of stone built by the hand of man; the temple of God is now his people. Jesus said that wherever there were two or three gathered together in his name, he would be there in the midst of them. Peter was there with two or three brethren from Joppa, and they all had the presence of the Holy Spirit. Cornelius knew this by revelation because God had already done a work in his heart. He knew he was in the presence of God. Is this not interesting? And there are still many people who lead meetings in temples made by man who tell people that they are coming supposedly to the house of God.

33 *Now therefore we are all here present before God to hear all things that are commanded thee of God.*

34 *Then Peter opened his mouth and said, Of a truth I perceive that God is no respecter of persons;*

35 *but in every nation he that fears him and works righteousness is acceptable to him.*

This is also interesting. The Jews had taught that people had to go to Jerusalem, be ceremoniously washed (this is where baptism comes from), be circumcised, and comply with many rituals in order to be accepted by God.

Here Peter was saying that it was enough to fear God and work righteousness (righteousness and justice are the same word in the original). Remember the message of John the Baptist to the soldiers who confronted him: *Oppress no one, neither accuse anyone falsely; and be content with your wages* (Luke 3:14). Neither did John tell them to leave the army. He did not tell them to resign.

> *For you to surrender to God it is not necessary to resign from your country, your people group, or your profession.*

For you to surrender to God it is not necessary to resign from your country, your people group, or your profession. It is necessary, however, to change the way you have been doing things, to learn the ways of the Lord. *In every nation he that fears him and works righteousness is acceptable to him* [God].

36 *The word which God sent unto the sons of Israel, preaching the gospel: peace by Jesus Christ (he is Lord of all),*

37 *that word, I say, ye know, which was published throughout all Judaea and began from Galilee, after the baptism which John preached,*

38 *how God anointed Jesus of Nazareth with the Holy Spirit and with power, who went about doing good and healing all that were oppressed of the devil, for God was with him.*

39 *And we are witnesses of all things which he did both in the land of Judea and in Jerusalem, whom they slew hanging him on a tree.*

40 *This same one God raised up the third day and showed him openly,*

41 *not to all the people, but unto witnesses chosen before of God, even to us, who ate and drank with him after he rose from the dead.*

42 *And he commanded us to preach unto the people and to testify that it is he who is ordained of God to be the Judge of living and dead.*

43 *Unto him all the prophets give witness, that whosoever believes in him shall receive remission of sins through his name.*

This is a simple gospel of telling who the Lord Jesus really is.

44 *While Peter yet spoke these words, the Holy Spirit fell on all those who heard the word.*

45 *And those of the circumcision who believed were astonished, as many as came with Peter, that also on the Gentiles the gift of the Holy Spirit was poured out.*

46 *For they heard them speak with tongues and magnify God.*

Today it is possible to go and hear people speaking in tongues in religious meetings, but the vast majority of the time no one hears God being magnified because no one understands anything. The tongues that were being spoken under the anointing of the Holy Spirit in the book of Acts were known languages (Acts 2:1-12). The people speaking in tongues by the Spirit did not previously know the language, but there were people around them who knew and could interpret and verified that what was being said magnified God.

The apostle Paul wrote to the Corinthian congregation:

1 Corinthians 14

27 *If anyone speaks in an unknown tongue, let it be by two, or at the most by three, and that by course; and let one interpret.*

28 *But if there is no interpreter, let him keep silence in the congregation {Gr. ekklesia – called out ones}, and let him speak to himself and to God.*

Why? Because if many are speaking in tongues and there is no interpretation, it will sound like the events at the Tower of Babel instead of the day of Pentecost. Also, with no interpretation and confirmation that this is an unknown language, it would be much harder to discern and weed out false spirits.

If someone were to come in and hear a message that magnified God in their native language from a person who did not know their language, they would be edified.

There are many spirits loose among those calling themselves Christians today that are doing what appear to be supernatural events. In many cases, these are not the real Holy Spirit. When this goes unchecked, the Holy Spirit becomes sad and begins to withdraw from a given individual or group. Where the Spirit of the Lord is, there is liberty – liberty to serve God, liberty to do the will of God. The fruit of the Spirit will be evident.

Peter and the other Jews were amazed when the true Holy Spirit fell over Cornelius and those in his house who were listening. They spoke with other tongues, but these were tongues that were understood. It was clear that they were magnifying God which confirmed that the real Holy Spirit had fallen on Cornelius and on his household and close friends.

The news of this real, supernatural event, however, caused quite a stir when Peter got back to Jerusalem. He had a lot of explaining to do about why he had fellowshipped and eaten with uncircumcised Gentiles. This controversy continued for some time until even Peter had to be corrected by Paul because he had been acting like a hypocrite. When alone with the Gentiles, he was fine, but if critical Jews were present he had been going back to his old ways.

The apostles did not have a meeting to decide how to fulfill the Great Commission

This serious controversy over implementation of the Jewish law continued, and God used the turmoil to further extend the gospel to the Gentiles. All of those walking in the center of the will of the Lord in this matter came under death threats from the Jews. This, in turn, helped produce and maintain a clean nucleus of believers that God multiplied all over the known world. Attacks and adversity came from all sides – sometimes from without, and sometimes from within.

The Jews continued to reject the gospel, and the Lord continued to offer the gospel to the Gentiles. Notice this: The apostles did not have a meeting to decide how to fulfill the Great Commission when Jesus declared that the gospel must be preached in all the world and that they were to be witnesses of him in Jerusalem, Judaea, Samaria, and unto the uttermost part of the earth (Acts 1:8). They did not strategize about who to send and how to go about it. Nothing like that is mentioned. God was moving them. It was the great persecution that caused the message to go out to Judaea and Samaria. Congregations formed and were multiplied by the power of the Holy Spirit.

Then God took an enemy of the gospel who was coordinating the persecution and truly converted him. He put Saul into real-life training by the Holy Spirit for almost fifteen years until the same Holy Spirit commissioned him as Paul, the apostle to the Gentiles.

Soon after Saul was converted, Barnabas wanted to introduce him to the apostles in Jerusalem, but they wanted nothing to do with him. God put it in the heart of Barnabas to befriend Paul, and they worked at Antioch until God decided to send both of them out as missionaries to the Gentiles.

Nowhere in the first ten chapters of the book of the Acts of the Apostles are elders appointed or named. The first mention of elders is after there was a famine in Jerusalem, and the Gentile congregations took up an offering and sent it to the elders. At the beginning of the book, elders are not mentioned, and when they are mentioned, they are simply there. The book of Acts does not give an exact explanation of how they came to be recognized, but the word *elder* has to do with "maturity" (the same word also translated as "perfection"). At the beginning of the new program that God was doing, no one had this maturity, but after fifteen or twenty years under the discipline of the Holy Spirit, elders in the congregation appeared, starting in Acts 11:30. It is only after Acts 14:23 that they are recognized or "ordained."

In a letter to Timothy, the apostle Paul describes elders and deacons. Many have read Paul's instructions to Timothy and Titus and have taken them as a license to name elders and deacons in congregations that they have started or that they somehow feel responsible for. This leads to a number of complications with highly gifted or trained individuals who are not yet mature and are not chosen directly by God but who then leaven the lump. True shepherds are those who will lay their lives down for the sheep.

The New Testament does not operate as law. It operates by grace and by faith. It is a trap for us to think that we can study the New Testament as if it were a book of law and then implement it with our own ability and understanding. This will never work. Unless God is directly involved, unless the Holy Spirit is presiding over every move, unless Jesus is pleased with the way in which we are operating, all our endeavors will be doomed as the enemy infiltrates our midst with what appear to be "angels of light."

For this reason, I am not in a hurry to name leadership. If there are material things to manage, sometimes it is necessary to designate responsibility. But regarding spiritual ministry, it is better for the Lord to do that. He is the only Mediator. He is the High Priest of the new covenant. He has all authority on heaven and on earth. He can place his hand, his discipline, and his seal over a specific person, and when he does this, it is obvious because the person operates from the heart of God. All we have to do is witness what God is doing and respect the authority that God has delegated. This was what Peter and the other apostles did regarding Paul.

There are many people with good hearts like Cornelius in many places, and God is no respecter of persons. The person who loves the truth and the light really loves Jesus who is the way, the truth, and the light, even if they may be confused at the start regarding history and terminology. When the Lord decides to clear things up for these people, he is not limited. God sent an angel to Cornelius, and the angel told him to call Peter. Is this not curious?

If God sent an angel to Cornelius, can he not send his angels anywhere and to anyone? But the Lord does not do everything through angels. In fact, there is a Scripture warning us about *spirits of error and doctrines of demons* [fallen angels] (1 Timothy 4:1). We are never instructed to pray to angels. We pray to the Lord, and he instructs his angels. God has his reasons for not ordering angels to share doctrine with us; he has ordered this to be done in a different manner through people like us who have been converted, selected by him, and demonstrate the fruit of the Holy Spirit.

Many think they have been converted, say they are converted, think they have the Holy Spirit, or say they have the Holy Spirit but are still planting confusion and not speaking of God with clarity. Therefore, people who follow God today must pass through a religious labyrinth where they hear many different voices in many places, and humans attempt to put themselves in the place of God, control others, and take what belongs to God for themselves or for their group.

God has permitted this for a time and for a season so the consequences of this might be demonstrated. But this is all going nowhere. The only way out of our present predicament is to stop everything and submit again to the Lord as Saul did. After Jesus stopped him, Saul did nothing; he did not even take a drink of water until the Lord sent someone to open his eyes and impart the real Holy Spirit.

The Lord Jesus told his disciples whom he had converted into apostles that he was leaving them a mission, but they had to wait first. Until they received power from on high, they were not to do anything. We cannot cause God to automatically do what we ordain. He does what he wants when he wants. If it seems the things that we want are not happening, we must stop acting without his orders and direction. There are always things that we can do.

Cornelius had spent years fearing God – with a soft, sensitive heart to pray and do what he could for others. After a time – we do not know how many months or years – an angel from God was sent to him. The angel came and pointed to Peter. Peter came and those of Cornelius' household were all filled with the Holy Spirit and placed into direct communion with God so the Lord could speak directly to them at any moment, guide them, work in and through them, and spread his work among the Jews and Gentiles.

The Lord did not randomly pick someone. He chose a Roman centurion who had a track record. Cornelius commanded troops in a very dangerous place. He worked for superiors who must have given him horrible orders from time to time and who desired to oppress the Jewish people. But he had spent years behaving in a manner that caught the attention of God, not only with his prayers but also with his acts of mercy (alms) until the time was right and the Lord sent an angel to him.

The things of God have inherent risks for everyone; this was a risk for Peter, and it was also a risk for the centurion. If we begin to walk with the Lord, the risk is great. In fact, we must risk everything. But the Lord does not command us to withdraw from the world. When Peter arrived, he did not tell Cornelius to withdraw from the army; in fact, Peter never mentioned the army. There were obviously other members of the Roman army present, and they too received the Holy Spirit. One of the soldiers had even gone on the mission to bring Peter.

As far as we know, the Holy Spirit did not tell any of these people that they needed to go to school or read the Bible more. No, it was sufficient to be filled with the Spirit. And it is interesting to note, that as time went by, there were Christian elders in Jerusalem. Elders? How? By following the Holy Spirit, the time came when individuals could be identified as having come to maturity in Christ; these people's lives could be held up as an example for others to follow. When a large offering was sent, it was delivered into their hands because there was no danger that they would use it for personal gain or fight over it. They could be trusted to use the money according to the leading of the Lord.

Let us pray:

Heavenly Father, may we see things from your perspective, may we share your priorities from the heart, may we not be respecters of persons, may we have discernment to identify the real Holy Spirit. We ask this in the name of our Lord Jesus. Amen.

CHAPTER 5

Our God is a Consuming Fire

*I came into my garden, my sister, my spouse: I have gath-
ered my myrrh and my spice; I have eaten my honeycomb
and my honey; I have drunk my wine and my milk: eat,
O friends; drink, beloved, drink abundantly.* [The quality
of her fruit can now be shared. He approves!]

*I sleep, but my heart watches for the voice of my beloved
that knocks at the door.* (Song of Solomon 5:1-2)

The Lord spoke of ten virgins (Matthew 25:1-13). They all
slept and had to be awakened. Five were prudent, and
when they woke up and trimmed their lamps, they had an
ample supply of oil in their vessels. These ten who slept soundly
and had to be awakened with a shout are not the bride. They
are virgins of Jerusalem, and some are prudent, and some are
foolish. The bride does not act like any of them. Even when she
sleeps, her heart watches.

He comes and says:

> 2 *Open to me, my sister, my love, my dove, my per-
> fect one: for my head is filled with dew, and my locks
> with the drops of the night.*

Things are coming along nicely *my perfect one!* This means that she lacks nothing (this is similar to the word *elder* mentioned in the previous chapter), but there is still one very important lesson that she must learn.

Look at the spontaneous reply from her heart:

> 3 *I have put off my coat; how shall I put it on? I have washed my feet; how shall I defile them?*

I have worked all day in the work of the Lord, and I am tired and have gone to bed. Even though my heart watches continually and my beloved is at the door, I want him to leave me in peace and let me have the rest I deserve.

Only three hundred men lapped the water with one hand while they watched and were vigilant

The test does not always come when we think it will. Most of Gideon's army was disqualified because they did not know how to drink the water. They knelt down and scooped up as much as they could with both hands. Only three hundred men lapped the water with one hand while they watched and were vigilant (Judges 7).

We can be doing very well with the Lord and think we deserve a little rest and vacation when the Lord comes knocking at the door. Many times the Lord sends someone to represent him, for he says that if we even give a glass of water to one of the least of his brethren, we have done it unto him. So we do not always know who may arrive at a very inconvenient time representing the Lord (Matthew 25:34-40). This is to discover what is really in our hearts. She is in a state where she lacks nothing. He refers to her as *my perfect one*. She is full of grace, gifts, and wisdom, but she still has to be proven in the most unlikely moment.

> 4 *My beloved put in his hand by the hole of the door, and my bowels were moved for him.*

But she hesitated just a bit too long.

> 5 *I rose up to open to my beloved, and my hands*
> *dripped with myrrh, and my fingers with sweet*
> *smelling myrrh, upon the handles of the lock.*

Even though she is identified in the way of the cross, the Lord still respects her will. The *handles of the lock* are only on the inside. He will not force them from the outside.

> 6 *I opened to my beloved, but my beloved had with-*
> *drawn himself and was gone; my soul went after*
> *his speech; I sought him, but I could not find him; I*
> *called him, but he gave me no answer.*

This was not like the last time when she had flat-out refused to go with him and hid in the wine cellar. She had only delayed slightly while thinking, "I really do not want to get up now." Then she thought better of it, but it was too late. He was seeing what the spontaneous reaction of her heart would be.

He must make sure that the spontaneous reaction of her heart will be the same as the spontaneous reaction of his heart in the face of any inconvenient circumstance or emergency. Jesus walked here on earth with his heart in perfect tune with the heart of his heavenly Father. He was even willing to lay down his life when this was required.

Paul wrote to Timothy that he was to *be instant in season and out of season.* We are to be ready even when it does not seem to be a likely time or occasion (2 Timothy 4:2-4).

Now she must go on another terrible search at night because when the Lord is not with us, it is night. When are we to work? In the day, because he says that when the night comes, we cannot work (John 9:4-5). We can do nothing without him no matter how gifted or talented we may be. At the end of the book of Revelation, there is no longer any need for the sun because he is permanently there in the city, and it is never night. Great sectors of the church do not seem to understand this.

> 7 *The watchmen that went about the city found me, they smote me, they wounded me; the keepers of the walls took away my outer cloak from me.*

This time, when she ran into the watchmen, it did not go so well. There are two possibilities here: Sometimes the watchmen are corrupt and attempt to discipline, control, rape, or even kill the bride. The other explanation is that when we make the same mistake the second time, the consequences will be much more painful. Both may apply.

> 8 *I charge you, O virgins of Jerusalem, if ye should find my beloved that ye cause him to know how sick I am with love.*

She is surer than ever that she loves him and only him, and she has to find him. Peace must reign in all things, and I do not trust in those who come with predictions or prophecies if this does not go along with what God has placed in my heart. If we have the peace that passes understanding, the Lord gives us a lot of range and liberty. But in the moment when we have no peace, we must seek him, for if we attempt to do anything without his peace, the consequences will be very serious. We could become disqualified and joined to the company of another who has no intimate contact with him.

Now the virgins of Jerusalem get involved. Why does it have to be him? Why can it not be another? Why can you not be satisfied with this group? Or with what is going on over there? Here comes the answer from God: It is the description of him through her eyes.

> 9 *What is thy beloved more than another beloved, O thou fairest among women? What is thy beloved more than another beloved that thou dost so charge us?*

The virgins recognize who she is and they want to know why she is so interested and fixed on him. Why does it have to be him directly? Why will some other ministry not suffice?

10 *My beloved is white and ruddy; the standard-bearer among the ten thousands.*

11 *His head is as the most fine gold, his locks are bushy and black as a raven.*

This is all very important. He is holy, yet down to earth. He has all power and authority (*the standard-bearer*). The mind of Jesus Christ is the mind of God. His bushy, black locks remind us that our ways are not God's ways (God's ways look black to us).

12 *His eyes are as doves by the rivers of waters.*

His sight is of the Spirit of God, and he is the only one who can satisfy.

12 *washed with milk, as doves that are next to abundance.*

13 *His cheeks are as a bed of aromatic spices, as fragrant flowers; his lips like lilies, dripping sweet smelling myrrh that transcends.*

The way of the cross is the only way to transcend our old nature. He reeks of wholesomeness and of unlimited capability.

14 *His hands are as gold rings set with beryls; his belly is as bright ivory overlaid with sapphires.*

Gold rings (divine authority) set with beryls (emeralds) associate justice with the throne of God. His belly (appetite) lines up with the throne of God. Ivory overlaid with sapphires is perfection. The sapphires or diamonds can split light into the seven colors of the rainbow. This is living water coming out of the belly that will cleanse and heal anyone he desires to help, instead of the corruption that flows out of the natural man that spews injustice, decay, and ruin. This is why she has to have him. No one else will do.

> 15 *His legs are as pillars of marble set upon sockets of fine gold.*

The two brass columns of the temple are called Jachin ("the Lord establishes") and Boaz ("only in him is there strength"). His pillars are not made out of brass (judgment). They are made out of marble in sockets of gold (beauty and strength symbolizing the transformation of man into the new nature). He is a man who walks in the nature of God.

> 15 *his countenance is as Lebanon, chosen as the cedars.*

Lebanon means "white mountain" (Hermon or Sion). This is where God commands the blessing and eternal life (Psalm 133:3; Deuteronomy 4:48). Those who look upon his face will never be the same; they will either be transformed or destroyed.

> 16 *His mouth is most sweet; he is altogether lovely. This is my beloved, and this is my friend, O virgins of Jerusalem.*

It is through an error of hesitation on her part which caused her to miss his invitation that leads to this ministry to the *virgins of Jerusalem.* She is not going to be defeated or dejected. She will use this opportunity and the urgency of the occasion to deeply challenge the virgins. Soon they desire to find him too!

Song of Solomon 6

> 1 *Where has thy beloved gone, O thou fairest among women? where didst thy beloved separate himself? that we may seek him with thee.*

It is very important in this transition that she describe him as he is. Notice that she does not *cast* [her] *pearls before swine* or *give ... that which is holy unto the dogs.* She is sharing this with other virgins. Her quest becomes a tremendous ministry, and all of a sudden, she knows where he is!

> 2 *My beloved is gone down into his garden, to the*
> *beds of spices, to feed in the gardens, and to gather*
> *the lilies.*

Where did she find him? In his garden. This is where Jesus loved to go while he was here on earth. Even after his resurrection, a lady found him in a garden (John 20:15). What does a garden represent? Our heart can be a garden where he loves to plant and uproot and cultivate until the fruit and spices

Our heart can be a garden where he loves to plant and uproot and cultivate

are pleasing to him. If we have lost or missed his presence, he may be present in the heart (garden) of another faithful person. This is where she found him with all the virgins of Jerusalem! Now she receives an even deeper revelation:

> 3 *I am my beloved's, and my beloved is mine; he*
> *feeds among the lilies.*

She has inverted the phrase that she pronounced in 2:16. Instead of saying *My beloved is mine,* she says, *I am my beloved's.* She understands that first she belongs to him and because of this, he belongs to her. He feeds among the lilies! She knew from the start that we need him to feed us, but now she understands that he also needs us! There are no more separations. Look at his description of her!

> 4 *Thou art beautiful, O my love, as Tirzah, as desir-*
> *able as Jerusalem, imposing as the standard-bearer*
> *of the army.*

This has intimate implications. *Tirzah,* meaning "delight" (Joshua 17:3), was one of the first women in Israel to receive an inheritance in her own right, but she had to agree to marry within the tribe of Judah. *Judah* means "praise." He is the lion of the tribe of Judah. The inheritance that she will receive is him. In the days before modern communications, the standard-bearer had the trumpet and essential control over the army. He is the standard-bearer, but she inherits him! He says that she is as imposing as the standard-bearer!

> 5 *Turn away thine eyes from me, for they have overcome me.*

Now he is the one who cannot live without her!

> 10 *Who is she that shows herself forth as the morning, fair as the moon, clear as the sun, and imposing as the standard-bearer of the army?*

Is she the herald of a new day in God? Does this describe a bride without spot or wrinkle or any such thing? Is Jesus going to return for a bride like this? He sounds motivated.

> 11 *I went down into the garden of nuts to see the fruits of the valley, and to see whether the vines flourished, and the pomegranates budded.*

The pomegranate is the fruit that is interwoven with the next stage beyond that of the flower, beyond the lily. The pomegranate is prominent in the Holy of Holies while the lily dominates the Holy Place. This is the time when the righteousness and justice of God will be openly manifest to his people. This is when the Lord prepares to make a most important change.

When she comes out of the desert like pillars of smoke, smelling of all the aromatic spices, with a tremendous anointing, and is represented by the bed or palanquin of Solomon, she is the vehicle and bears the glory of God. The Lord is using this to accomplish his purposes and to have a bride who is *instant in season and out of season.* He desires one whose thoughts do not center on herself, not even when she is resting or thinks that she deserves something for all that she has sacrificed and accomplished for him. Not until she is no longer focused on herself can she focus on the fruit that pleases the Lord. She lives to make him happy.

She has left the realm of the gifts as the fruit comes forth, and as that fruit comes to maturity, it can be reproduced, resulting in more generations. The promise of blessing from generation to generation of fathers to sons has never been fulfilled among the people of God. Until now when a generation has served God, their children or grandchildren or great grandchildren have turned their backs on the Lord. This happened back in ancient Jerusalem, and the same thing has occurred throughout the long and checkered history of the church. Only on very rare occasions and on a very small scale have the children and the children of their children followed in the faith of their fathers, but this is what has to happen. If we are successful in ministry, our children must surpass us; there are only a few examples.

Joshua went above and beyond Moses. Elijah went above and beyond Elisha. Jesus went way beyond John the Baptist. We do have a few examples, but now God wants this to happen with all his people.

Amos 8

1 *Thus hath the Lord GOD showed unto me: and behold a basket of summer fruit.*

2 *And he said, Amos, what seest thou? And I said, A basket of summer fruit. Then said the LORD unto me, The end is come upon my people of Israel; I will not again pass over them any more.*

3 *And the cantors of the temple shall howl in that day, said the Lord GOD; there shall be many dead bodies in every place; they shall cast them forth with silence.*

God cancelled the Passover, and judgment came upon Israel because their basket of fruit was not what he was looking for. God told Jeremiah that Jerusalem would be spared if there was just one righteous man in the city. There was not!

Jesus mused, "When the son of man returns, will he find faith upon the earth?"

In the stage of the blade of grass that comes forth, we know not how, and even in the stage of the flower, the lily represents the gifts of the Spirit; God will allow us to continue if we agree with him and make a good-faith effort to convince him that we desire to follow him and that he may deal with us as he sees fit. But when the fruit comes forth, it is a different story. The tares must be plucked up, bundled, and burned. Only the wheat will be harvested into his "barn." God will not "pass over" tares and thorns and briers among his people once they have come to maturity.

She is now coming out of the desert of special preparations and dealings of God. The church age is ending. She is about to cross over the Jordan River and enter into her inheritance. She is producing the fruit that he desires. By the Spirit, he is inspecting her garden (the gardens of the hearts of the priesthood of all believers), and this is what he says!

12 *Or ever I was aware, my soul made me return
like the chariots of Amminadib.*

This is the only instance of Amminadib in Scripture. There are several uses of Amminadab (which means "my people are willing"), as in when Deborah and Barak sang: *Praise ye the LORD ... the people willingly offered themselves.* They were willing to lay down their lives for the Lord on the field of battle, and they sang about why Reuben, Dan, and Asher did not show up that day (Judges 5). But for those who did go forth with Deborah and Barak, it says that even the stars fought from their courses.

For this people who are eager to lay down their lives, who are instant in season and out of season, who do not hesitate when invited to go forth with their Lord, God's desires flow in their hearts by his very nature. They do not have to think about it. They do not have to seek visions of confirmation. They do not need testimony or confirmation from others. Their hearts are pure, and even when they sleep, their hearts are watching.

On a faraway occasion, long ago, he knocked, but they were not ready; after their agonizing, desperate nighttime search for him, they will never again be separated. What he asks and what he is flows instantly from their hearts. This is the fruit he has been longing for. This is what he has been yearning for ever since Adam and Eve disappointed him in the garden.

> *Something is about to happen that has never been seen before.*

Jesus said he does not know the day or the hour of his return, only the Father knows (Matthew 24:36). The Father has the ultimate responsibility to prepare the bride.

When the sublime beauty, excellent character, and unsurpassed fruit of the bride meet Jesus' expectations, he will exclaim:

> 12 *Or ever I was aware, my soul made me return like the chariots of Amminadib.*

This is nothing less than the return of our Lord for his bride who has no spot or wrinkle or any such thing!

When she rises out of the wilderness like pillars of smoke (Song of Solomon 3:6), she is compared with Solomon's palanquin (she is the vehicle to transport God's glory). We have had this with those who have allowed God to cleanse and use them throughout the long history of the church. But now we are entering another day. Something is about to happen that has never been seen before. God will come to his people in a way that we have not even been able to imagine.

Instead of us being the vehicle to transport the glory of God, he will be the vehicle for us. There are several examples of this in Scripture. David wanted to build God a house, but God said that he was going to build David a house (2 Samuel 7). When God called Gideon, Scripture does not say that the Spirit of God covered Gideon. The language is reversed. It literally implies that the Spirit of God went forth dressed as Gideon (Judges 6:34).

We have attempted to do everything we can think of for the Lord, but we have not managed to build the temple of living stones, and we have not yet seen the unlimited glory of God. It would destroy the natural man. Now God is going to build a house for us. We are going to ride in his chariot!

We have had the natural man inside, and he has covered us with his Spirit while he worked on our nasty insides. Now, however, he desires to put his finished work on display. It will be his nature inside and it will only look like us outside. There will be two witnesses: him and her. They will both be on the same page. They will both be saying the same thing:

Revelation 22

17 *And the Spirit and the bride say, Come. And let him that hears say, Come. And let him that is thirsty come; and whosoever will, let him take of the water of life freely.*

He will be the vehicle to take her to examine the gardens; this is the secret to redeeming all of creation. All creation groans and travails for this moment (Romans 8:14-24).

Song of Solomon 6

13 *Return, return, O Shulamite; return, return, that we may look upon thee. What will ye see in the Shulamite? She shall be as a multitude of tabernacles.*

This is the Feast of Tabernacles. This is God dwelling (tabernacling) with his people. Jesus said that if his disciples had seen him, they had also seen his Father. Jesus will come back and sweep his bride off her feet. Those who see her will see Jesus. They will yearn to see her.

Song of Solomon 7

> 1 *How beautiful are thy feet in thy shoes, O prince's daughter!*

Moses and Joshua had to take off their shoes because they were on holy ground (Exodus 3:5; Joshua 5:15). They had to take off all man-made preparation in order to learn to do things God's way. This bride is a little girl who started out barefoot, burned by the sun and tending goats, and now she is shod with the preparation of the gospel of peace. She is going to present the gospel his way, not the way people are trained in some Bible school, seminary, or discipleship course. She has received this preparation because she has walked with him until she has passed the test.

At this point, she finally has it straight (Song of Solomon 2:16, 6:3).

> 10 *I am my beloved's, and with me he has his contentment.*

She has received the inheritance, and it is him. Now she knows she belongs to him and his contentment is her. She will always conduct herself in such a manner as to keep him content. Because she has everything, her focus is not on herself or on taking things to herself. She is granted another invitation.

> 11 *Come, my beloved, let us go forth into the field;*
> *let us lodge in the villages.*

> 12 *Let us get up early to the vineyards; let us see*

*if the vines flourish, whether the tender flowers
appear, if the pomegranates bud forth; there I will
give thee my loves.*

This is truly an unending love story. All creation will be redeemed. There will be *new heavens and a new earth in which dwells righteousness* (2 Peter 3:13).

Hebrews 12

22 *but ye are come unto Mount Sion and unto the city
of the living God, the heavenly Jerusalem, and to an
innumerable company of angels,*

23 *to the congregation of the called out ones of the first-
born, who are registered in the heavens and to God the
Judge of all and to the spirits of just men made perfect*

24 *and to Jesus, the mediator of the new testament and
to the blood of sprinkling, that speaks better than that
of Able.*

25 *See that you do not refuse him that speaks. For if
those who refused him that spoke on earth did not
escape, much less shall we escape, if we turn away from
him that speaks from the heavens,*

26 *whose voice then shook the earth; but now he has
promised, saying, Yet even once, I shall shake not the
earth only, but also the heaven.*

27 *And this word, Yet even once, signifies the removing of
those things that are shaken, as of things that are made,
that those things which cannot be shaken may remain.*

28 *Therefore, receiving a kingdom which cannot be
moved, let us hold fast to the grace, by which we serve
God, pleasing him with reverence and godly fear:*

29 *for our God is a consuming fire.*

The Mystery Revealed

The mysteries of God have two basic categories: (1) The mystery of iniquity (but this only has to do with two or three verses), and (2) the mystery or mysteries of the plans of God and how God is going to effect his plans to bring about his will (thirty-two verses speak of this).

One of the reasons this is a mystery to the natural man is that his spiritual senses are not functioning. Our senses are attached to our conscience. If our spiritual senses are not functioning, the function of our conscience will not be optimal. This is the part of our being where we not only know about the will of God, but we also feel what he is feeling. Our conscience serves to reprove us of sin but it also aids us to feel the approval of God when things are going well. When God receives us as sons (and this is not limited by gender) by the Spirit, we can exclaim, "Abba, Father." Every legitimate son who is engendered by God also receives the discipline of God, but we have the security that if we fail, he does not fail.

He will do everything possible to deliver us from our error. The jeopardy of every believer comes when we reject the correction of the Lord. He will not cast us out if we make a mistake. But if we commit errors with our eyes wide open, it will be extremely painful.

I searched and found thirty-five verses that contain the words *mystery* or *mysteries*. This is five times seven. Seven represents completion with nothing lacking. It refers to the day of the Lord, the Lord's rest, and the inheritance that the Lord has for us. When we rest from our own labors and enter into him, we are able to do the work of God. The work of God must first be effected in us in order for it to be effected through us. Seven is the number that represents all of this, and five is the number that symbolizes the grace of God which is the power of God to change us, to save us, and to do for us what we are unable to do for ourselves. It is unmerited favor, but it is also much, much more than that. This word *mystery* occurs in exactly thirty-five verses.

How the Lord will lead us, what the way of the Lord will be like, is a complete mystery to the natural man. It is impossible for man to be able to perceive the grace of God in his natural state without a touch from the Lord. It is necessary that the Lord send the evangelist, that the Lord send forth the Word, and that the Lord touch our understanding so we can understand how the gospel operates.

The apostle Paul says that the gospel is a mystery (Ephesians 6:19). God granted him the grace to go forth with the mystery of the gospel and to reveal it. In the letter to the Ephesians, it implies that someone sent from God may spread grace. Peter writes, *Grace and peace be multiplied unto you* (1 Peter 1:2; 2 Peter 1:2).

The first use of the word *mystery* in the Bible is in the book of Daniel. The king had a dream he could not remember, yet he knew it was important. So he called in all the wise men and magicians and demanded not only the interpretation, but that they first tell him the dream. If they told him the dream, he would remember, and he could also confirm that their interpretation was true.

We need to consider dreams and visions because they have to do with the mystery. Those who are asleep cannot understand, and in Ephesians it says, *Awake thou that sleepest ... and the Christ shall shine upon thee.* When we are asleep, we dream dreams; when we are asleep, dead in trespasses and sin, God has a dream inside of us that we are unable to remember. How is the image of God restored in us? What does God want to do? We have vague thoughts that our existence must have a purpose, but how?

> *We have democracies, and we have laws, but the people (clay) in their natural state cannot comply with the laws (iron).*

A vision is seen by someone who is awake. In a vision God can clear up a dream. Obviously it is necessary to have wisdom from God to be able to interpret these things, but visions are easier to interpret than dreams because the person is awake.

When the king called the wise men and magicians together, he wanted to know what the dream was and what the interpretation was. Daniel was going to be killed along with all the wise men of Babylon because no one could tell the king his dream.

Daniel 2

19 Then the mystery was revealed unto Daniel in a night vision.

God gave Daniel a vision to reveal what the king had dreamed. The dream of the king portrayed all the world empires that would come. He had seen a huge statue with a head of gold, arms and shoulders of silver, a belly of brass, legs of iron, and feet of iron mixed with clay. These represent all of man's systems of government from Babylon until now.

Man has apparent good intentions, and the king of Babylon was an absolute monarch. But the materials degrade from the head down to the feet, and the statue was unable to walk or function. We have democracies, and we have laws, but the people (clay) in their natural state cannot comply with the laws (iron). Then a huge stone cut without hands crashed into the feet of the image, turning it all to dust (which the wind scattered), and the stone grew into a huge mountain that covered all the earth. This is the future kingdom of God.

The Lord is preparing an event with that stone that he has been forming. That stone is Christ, and two thousand years ago it was one person. But now it is a body of Christ of many members of which the Lord Jesus is the Head. The mystery of the will of God is how God will change the nature of the human race. To make this change, God must take beings like us who are the clay that cannot mix with the iron of the law and cannot walk according to the ways of God, and transform us into the image that is described in Revelation 10 of the glorious Christ with his head in the heavens and his feet on the earth. There is no degradation of the materials, and this mystery turns into a ministry.

Two witnesses help reveal the mystery of what the will of God is. The word *witness* is exactly the same as the word *martyr* in Greek. Witnesses like this are capable of giving their very life for what they are living. Scripture mentions martyrs who never died a violent death. The apostle John is described with the same word *witness* as Jesus (Revelation 1:2, 5). According to tradition, John died of old age even though Scripture describes him as a witness (martyr). He lived his life as a faithful witness, and this is why he was exiled to the island of Patmos.

Peter was killed, but the Lord decided something different for John. Only the Lord knows what will happen, and sometimes the tests that we face are very subtle. The tests can be as simple as being asked to go on a trip or to go speak to someone .

In the parable of the sower, four types of ground (or hearts) are mentioned and this parable prompted a question from the disciples.

Matthew 13

10 *Then the disciples came and said unto him, Why dost thou speak unto them in parables?*

11 *He answered and said unto them, Because it is given unto you to know the mysteries of the kingdom of the heavens, but to them it is not given.*

Mark 4

11 *And he said unto them, Unto you it is given to know the mystery of the kingdom of God; but unto those that are without, all these things are done in parables.*

12 *that seeing they may see and not perceive, and hearing they may hear and not understand, lest at any time they should be converted, and their sins should be forgiven them.*

Luke 8:10 is similar. Jesus is quoting Isaiah who prophesied that there is a people that will not be converted by the Lord (Isaiah 6:9-10). Why? Because their hearts are not right. They did not prepare their hearts.

Proverbs 16

1 *Of man are the preparations of the heart, but the answer of the tongue is from the LORD.*

All the kings of Israel and Judah listed in 1 and 2 Chronicles or 1 and 2 Kings that got into trouble had problems that started in their hearts; they did not set their hearts to exclusively follow God.

Ephesians 2

8 *For by grace are ye saved through faith and that not of yourselves: it is the gift of God.*

9 *Not of works, lest any man should boast.*

The grace that saves us is not ours and neither is the faith. Scripture speaks of the faith of Christ, which must work in

> *The grace that saves us is not ours and neither is the faith.*

us. Our faith can get us to the altar where we must enter into covenant with him. Our faith can lead us to authorize the Lord to intervene in our lives. If we are sick, our faith in the doctor can get us to the hospital. The most that our faith in the doctor can accomplish is to lead us to sign on the dotted line and authorize the surgery. But we cannot perform open-heart surgery on ourselves. This must be conducted by the doctor.

Our faith and the faith of Christ must both work.

Ephesians 4

1 *I therefore, the prisoner of the Lord, beseech you that ye walk worthy of the vocation with which ye are called,*

Paul does not consider it to be a tragedy that he is a prisoner. He is *the prisoner of the Lord* and is glad to be found worthy to represent the Lord on such a special mission. I know how he must have felt after experiencing the same feeling when I had been taken hostage and put in prison on multiple occasions.

2 *with all humility and meekness, with tolerance, forbearing one another in love,*

3 *being diligent to guard the unity of the Spirit in the bond of peace.*

Those who suffer persecution for the cause of Christ will either become scarred and bitter, or the difficulties and adversity will produce *humility and meekness, with tolerance.* This is the same as the Shulamite who *rises out of the wilderness like pillars of smoke, perfumed with myrrh and frankincense and with all the aromatic powders.*

4 *There is one body and one Spirit, even as ye are called in one hope of your calling,*

There are many local congregations (or churches) but only one body. Scripture knows nothing about a "local body" which can then have a "local head or heads."

5 *one Lord, one faith, one baptism,*

6 *one God and Father of all, who is above all and through all, and in you all.*

God wants to bring this all together, and this is part of the mystery of his will. He is to work in us. It is *Christ in you, the hope of glory.* We are to become part of the body of Christ, and all are led and guided by the Head which is Jesus Christ. The Holy Spirit is the Spirit of the body that joins the entire body of Christ and unites us with all the other members of the same body.

Our own works cannot save us.

Ephesians 2

9 *Not of works, lest any man should boast.*

10 *For we are his workmanship, created in Christ Jesus for good works, which God has prepared that we should walk in them.*

If we are to enter into his grace, our faith must connect us to the faith of Christ, to the dependency that Jesus Christ had on his Father, to do the will of his Father. When one of the disciples desired to see the Father, Jesus replied, "If you have seen me, you have seen the Father." He did not come to do anything different from the Father.

Our purpose and vocation mentioned in Ephesians is that we become worthy representatives of God and that others see Christ in us. Note that when we fail, God can recover our ministry if we remain docile to him. The world needs living examples of humility and repentance. We must acknowledge our failures and repent when necessary, for without the power of God inside of us, it is not even possible to repent in the biblical sense of the word. Repentance is not alligator tears. It is a 180-degree course reversal. It is not enough to be sad and sorry; we must cease and desist.

This type of repentance in us stimulates the faith of others so they desire to depend completely on the Lord also. All of this is a mystery to those who are still outside, not born again, and cannot see in the realm of the Spirit. But all these people still have the dream deep down inside. They were all created in the image and likeness of God, but because of the fall, they are all asleep.

The Lord must send forth a Daniel to remind them of their dream, give them the revelation of the dream, and tell them the purpose of God in creating us and his plans for this fallen creation. Man has a *head of gold* with seemingly good intentions, *arms and shoulders of silver* in his desire to rescue and help others, but he also has a *belly of bronze* and is terribly judgmental of others. Man has one standard for others and quite another for himself. He condemns his enemies but justifies the same conduct for himself and his friends.

If we lie, it is because our enemies lie, and we must not let them win. If we commit injustice, it is because others were unjust first, and we must combat them, and so on with everything. In this manner, we can easily wind up worse than our enemies.

This is called an eye for an eye and a tooth for a tooth, which, if allowed to continue, could leave everyone blind and toothless!

The true gospel is a mystery to anyone who has not received revelation from God. What some call the Apocalypse is really the revelation of Jesus Christ. All they see are plagues and destruction. But it is only destruction to the natural, carnal man. It ends with a beautiful, clean city that descends, and God lives together with his people. In this city is a river of life, clear as crystal that is the exact opposite of many of the rivers we know which have many tributaries and only one outlet. God's river has one source and distributes his grace, mercy, and peace everywhere.

In Eden the river of God flowed into four branches onto all the earth, but now due to the law of gravity, rivers do not flow like this. According to Ezekiel, the river of God begins with waters that are not very deep. They get deeper and deeper as you follow the river until there are *waters to swim in* (Ezekiel 47:2-5). Many beautiful trees grow on the banks. In Eden only one tree of life grew, but in Revelation 22 the tree of life is on each side of the river, everywhere. It gives fruit every month, and the leaves are for the healing of the Gentiles.

The Lord desires to place his nature in each one of us that we may be *trees of righteousness, the planting of the LORD,* and that we may bear the fruit of righteousness which only happens when he is planted deep inside of us (Isaiah 61:1-3).

Ephesians 4

6 *one God and Father of all, who is above all and through all, and in you all.*

7 *But unto each one of us is given grace according to the measure of the gift of the Christ.*

The gift is Christ. The Father gave his Son.

John 3

16 *For God so loved the world that he gave his only begotten Son, that whosoever believes in him should not perish but have eternal life.*

There is no salvation apart from him. He is our health, he is our hope, and he is our salvation. God's plan of redemption is to incorporate us into himself.

We must become part of him, part of the body of Christ which has many members.

Reconciliation with Christ is not meeting him halfway. It is not abandoning the more deadly sins while retaining the venial ones. Reconciliation is to be holy as he is holy.

Matthew 5

48 *Be ye therefore perfect, even as your Father who is in the heavens is perfect.*

He would not give us this order if it were not possible. The children of Israel got into a lot of trouble with a secondhand revelation. They refused to continue to hear the voice of God. They sent Moses instead (Exodus 20:19). This is how they got a covenant written on tablets of stone instead of on the tablets of their hearts. If his Word is to change our hearts, we must hear directly from him, for he desires to write his laws on the tablets of our hearts and in our minds (Proverbs 3:1-6; Jeremiah 31:33; Hebrews 8:10). He wants to deal with each one of us directly.

I want to share about the mystery of the gospel, which is his will in us, if you are able to receive it. Pray that the Lord will open the eyes of your understanding to receive this because it is extremely important.

Ephesians 4

8 *Therefore he saith, When he ascended up on high, he led captivity captive and gave gifts unto men.*

What kind of gifts did he give? The Spirit is the earnest (down payment) on our inheritance. It is not the fullness of our inheritance in Christ. Without the Spirit, we cannot enter; we are without the grace of God and without the power of God. Without faith, it is impossible to please God

we all fall into the same trap of wanting to decide what is good and what is evil for ourselves.

(Hebrews 11:6). And we can think that we have some of this, but the fullness is in him. Unless we remain connected to him, we will never have the fullness of God in us, and we will never receive the inheritance.

The Devil thought that he would kill the first man and his wife because he did not want to be subject to them. He worked out a very astute plan so God would have to kick them out of the garden, and they would become subject to death and eventually die. What happened to the first man, Adam, when he lost his direct attachment to God? He had a problem; he lost his authority and transmitted the problem to all his descendants (us).

As soon as we become conscious of our existence and begin to exercise our will, we all fall into the same trap of wanting to decide what is good and what is evil for ourselves. Even in the most lucid moments of the natural man when he is contemplating how to regain his lost fellowship with God, his thoughts focus on returning the knowledge of evil to God. He is sometimes willing to let God tell him what is evil, but it never even occurs to him to return the knowledge of good. So we continue with many things that are "good" to us but are not good in the eyes of God. This is why we have so many houses full of altars and images. They think this is good. Also, those who focus their time and energy on the things of this world are convinced they are seeking "good" things and not harming anyone.

We might be seeking a long life and have certain criteria in a certain context, but the worst form of deception is when we are doing something that we think is fine, but God does not agree. This is why the human race has not been able to leave the curse behind and enter into the blessing.

The most disturbing thing to me about the parable of the sower and the four types of ground (hearts) is not those with the hard, impenetrable ground; the stony, shallow ground does not bother me so much either. This is somewhat to be expected. What bothers me are those who receive the seed, it begins to develop, it grows and grows, but as time passes, that plant never produces good fruit because the thorns and thistles of the cares of this world choke it.

This is a problem that resides in the very nature of the ground. Look what happened in the curse:

Genesis 3

17 *cursed shall be the ground for thy sake; in sorrow shalt thou eat of it all the days of thy life;*

18 *thorns also and thistles shall it bring forth to thee*

Due to the sin of Adam and Eve when they chose the Tree of the Knowledge of Good and Evil instead of the Tree of Life, the cursed ground will always bring forth thorns and thistles. Even if good seed is planted, man will have to cultivate it by the sweat of his brow until he returns to the dust from which he was taken. And if we are ever to bring forth good fruit in the kingdom of God, if the quality of the grain that we bring forth is ever going to be the same quality as the seed that was planted, we must die (Galatians 2:20). Remember that the Lord Jesus is the grain of wheat that fell into the ground and died (John 12:24) so that his life and virtue could come forth in us. We need to pay attention to how the passage in Ephesians continues:

Ephesians 4

7 But unto each one of us is given grace according to the measure of the gift of the Christ.

8 Therefore he saith, When he ascended up on high, he led captivity captive and gave gifts unto men.

When Jesus died and descended into hades, the Devil's jail, he not only broke free and took the keys of death from the Devil, but he also ascended, taking with him all who were his, such as Abraham and all the patriarchs. Remember the parable of Lazarus and the rich man (Luke 16:19-31). Lazarus, Abraham, and the wicked rich man were all locked up in hades, but there were two compartments with a great gulf between them. Abraham and Lazarus were on one side receiving special treatment, and the rich man was on the other side in torment. When Jesus descended into hades, he took *captivity captive*; he took those who were his and who were awaiting redemption and left those who were not his.

7 But unto each one of us is given grace according to the measure of the gift of the Christ.

8 Therefore he saith, When he ascended up on high, he led captivity captive and gave gifts unto men.

9 (Now that he ascended, what is it but that he also descended first into the lower parts of the earth?

10 He that descended is the same also that ascended up far above all the heavens, that he might fulfill all things.)

Brethren, this is a central part of *The Mystery of the Will of God* in us, the mystery of the gospel. When the Lord Jesus died, he descended into hades; he broke the jail of the Devil, and he ascended on high with the ability to give gifts to us. He himself is the gift! Now he comes to us by the Holy Spirit, but he shall return one day in person for his bride.

When he gave the Spirit, the Spirit came to manifest Christ in us. But we all come to the Lord asking for help. When we feel exhausted, when we feel trapped, when there seems to be no way out, this is the perfect time to receive the Lord. It is when we fear death or are in danger of losing health, livelihood, or loved ones that it seems like a good idea to surrender to him. This is part of the gospel. It says that he descended into the lower parts of the earth. What are we? Dust of the earth. He wants to enter into the deepest parts of our being and change our appetites, change our heart, and purify our heart. The pure in heart shall see God! (Matthew 5:8).

He comes to break the prison in which we have been captive

He does not leave us in the lower parts of the earth, but this is where we have failed. We have had it all wrong. We have thought that it is enough to return the knowledge of evil and to let him come into our lives and correct that which is evil. But he has a different idea of what is good. He did not remain in hades after he broke the power of death, took the keys, broke the prisoners who were his out of jail, and placed them in liberty. He did not leave them in the depths of the earth. He did not remain down there having his party. No, he took them captive to righteousness and ascended. This is what the church has not understood.

He does not come to do our will. He does not come to be our slave. He comes to place his order into our being. He comes to break the prison in which we have been captive so we may become like Paul, prisoners of the Lord. And if he descends into the most profound depths of this earth where we are, it is because he is going to ascend afterward and take us with him by the Spirit *far above all the heavens.*

He that descended is the same also that ascended up far above all the heavens, that he might fulfill all things. There was a piece missing to our understanding of the gospel. He can, in a moment in time, put us into direct contact with God the Father. Then, whatsoever we desire to ask in his name will be granted if our heart is one with his heart. This is what it says in the gospel of John. And we still have brethren asking for a Mercedes Benz, a private jet, and a great hacienda because they have not understood the name of the Lord, the nature of the Lord.

According to the name of the Lord, according to the nature of the Lord, when we are pure in heart, it is only necessary to seek first the kingdom of God and his righteousness (Matthew 6:33). It is not necessary to ask for the things of this world. The Lord can easily supply all our needs. He seeks a people who will ask for the real riches. The letter to the Ephesians mentions the riches of his glory and his grace. There are riches of his grace, and we can form part of his jewels.

Malachi 3

17 *And they shall be mine, said the LORD of the hosts, in that day when I make up my jewels; and I will spare them, as a man spares his own son that serves him.*

This context of the mystery of the will of God will be revealed. Where? In us! He descended into the lower parts of the earth – first the natural and then the spiritual – *that he might fulfill all things.*

1 Corinthians 15

45 *And so it is written, The first man Adam was*

made a living soul; the last Adam was made a life-giving Spirit.

46 Howbeit the spiritual is not first, but the natural; and afterward, that which is spiritual.

He fulfilled all things, but he desires to fulfill them again in each one of us by descending into our earth and taking us with him far above all heavens into the inheritance of the sons of God. It is in this context that he says in Ephesians 4:

11 And he gave some, apostles; and some, prophets; and some, evangelists; and some, pastors and teachers,

These ministries are not a clerical category of people, of rulers over the church who will replace the Head that is him. This is the normal standard for all believers. After he takes us far above all the heavens, he desires to send us forth to accomplish the will of God and edify what God is doing by involving us in *good works, which God has prepared that we should walk in them.*

What is an apostle? He is someone who represents another, an ambassador who will build according to the ways of the Lord. We have not understood the spheres of authority because the Lord can send someone forth in a limited context. For many years, the Lord sent me forth to do some things and not others. For many years, the Lord allowed me to preach where I was invited, but he did not allow me to start a group or be directly responsible for one. For many years, I had to work under the responsibility of other leaders who sometimes were very imperfect. I had to shoulder the load with a willing heart to make sure things worked out even when I thought that I had a better idea.

The Lord says that the one who is faithful with little will be given more, and the one who is not faithful with little will lose what he thinks he has. The faithful one is the real apostle.

He is the real prophet. He is the real evangelist. He is the real pastor and teacher. If our heart is clean, he can work through us. This is not for a select few. This is within the reach of all the people of God if we have the faith to appropriate it.

In the Old Testament, there was anointing for three classes of people: prophets, priests, and kings. In the new covenant, he *has made us* [all] *kings and priests unto God* (Revelation 1:6). It is possible that any person who has the Spirit of God may prophesy *for the testimony of Jesus is the spirit of prophecy* (Revelation 19:10). Prophecy is not guessing the future. It is speaking clean words of God instead of our own.

> 11 *And he gave some, apostles; and some, prophets; and some, evangelists; and some, pastors and teachers,*
>
> 12 *for the perfecting of the saints in the work of the ministry, unto the edifying of the body of the Christ*
>
> 13 *until we all come forth in the unity of the faith and of the knowledge of the Son of God unto a perfect man, unto the measure of the coming of age of the Christ:*

Some translations attempt to make sense of this by translating it "unto the fullness of the stature of Christ," but this text actually refers to the Jewish concept of coming to maturity at age thirty, so they might receive the fullness of the inheritance of their father. When Jesus was about thirty years of age, he was baptized. The heavens were opened, and the fullness of the Spirit descended upon him as a dove (John 1:32). He received the Spirit, the fullness of the inheritance of his real Father without measure (John 3:34).

His real Father was not Joseph the carpenter who had adopted him and had done a wonderful job of raising him as an example for us. Why did Jesus receive the inheritance from his heavenly Father, and why does he want us to become like him?

14 *That we no longer be children, tossed to and fro
and carried about with every wind of doctrine, by
the sleight of men and cunning craftiness, by which
they lie in wait to deceive,*

15 *but following the truth in charity, let us grow up
into him in all things, who is the head, the Christ:*

Maturity is indispensable. When a grain of wheat comes
to maturity (and in Greek and Hebrew, the word *maturity* is
the same word that is translated "perfection"), it is viable. This
means that you can plant it, and it will grow and bring forth
the same quality. If you attempt to plant an immature grain of
wheat that is still in the milk stage, it will not sprout.

This is what we have done when we take a group of young
people, give them a six-week course, and send them out to preach
what we think is the gospel, but it is a disaster. I remember
being involved in an "evangelistic" campaign in a remote town
which was sponsored by two groups, one that trained young
people and the other that worked with businessmen. When we
returned a few months later, the married leader of the group of
businessmen had run off with the female director of the young
people. Two households had been destroyed, and the overall
effect was worse than if we had never had any meetings.

This happens when we send people forth or people feel they
should go forth, and God did not send them.

Another time when I went to a camp or base that was training young people with short courses on "evangelism," not only
were the young people messed up, but even the staff was way
off base.

The seed they were attempting to plant was not mature,
and they did not understand that we are the seed, and the
seed is in the fruit. If our lives do not demonstrate the fruit of
the Holy Spirit, we have no incorruptible seed to plant. Those
whose personal lives are not in order, but they force others to

accept their four points and repeat a prayer, plant a corruptible gospel. The Holy Spirit has not really separated them for this work. When Paul and Barnabas were separated and sent out by the Holy Spirit from the congregation at Antioch, they were among the most mature individuals in the group.

Maturity means that nothing is lacking. The seed is viable and can be planted. It will grow and reproduce the same quality. This is the definition of perfection in the Bible, but it has been greatly misunderstood. The biblical definition of perfection has nothing to do with getting 100 percent on every math test. It does not mean that we will no longer have normal human limitations in which we are prone to honest mistakes. It is perfection of the heart, and this is a different realm.

> *The biblical definition of perfection has nothing to do with getting 100 percent on every math test.*

Those who are perfect or mature in this sense can live with a clean conscience before God and man and in victory over known sin. They are not in rebellion against God, and they are not hiding secret sin (iniquity) in their hearts. The goal and direction of their lives is to fulfill the will of God.

This has to do with the Greek word *hamartia,* one of several words translated "sin" in the New Testament. It does not mean to miss the mark. It describes the archer who would shoot at the wrong target. If in the heat and confusion of the battle he were to take a pot shot at someone on his own side whom he had a grudge against, it would be hamartia even if he missed. And if some of the shots taken at the real enemy missed, this was not considered hamartia because he was consistently shooting at the right target even if he did not always hit the bull's-eye. If the archer shot one of his own men by mistake, this would not be hamartia either, because the intention of his heart was upright even though his hand slipped. Let us consider the following Scripture in this light:

— 107 —

1 John 3

6 *Whosoever abides in him does not sin* [hamartia]: *whosoever sins has not seen him or known him.*

Now look at this:

Matthew 7

22 *Many will say to me in that day, Lord, Lord, have we not prophesied in thy name? and in thy name have cast out devils? and in thy name done many wonderful works?*

23 *And then I will profess unto them, I never knew you.*

The person who continues to pursue the wrong goals after claiming to know the Lord does not really know the Lord. To know something about the Lord and to actually know the Lord are two entirely different things. For this communion of the presence of the Lord, we cannot enter unilaterally with our own will. God must open a door. We can open the door for him to correct what needs to be rectified in us. The two things need to function together just like a good marriage and this is why he now applies this mystery to marriage.

There is a realm in which whosoever will may come and whosoever calls upon the Lord shall be saved, but that does not necessarily mean that all these people will reign and rule with Christ as his bride.

Colossians 1

26 *even the mystery which has been hid from ages and from generations, but now is made manifest to his saints,*

27 *to whom God would make known what is the riches of the glory of this mystery in the Gentiles, which is Christ in you, the hope of glory.*

CHAPTER 7

The Mystery as Seen in Marriage

God's open door and our response must function together just like a good marriage, and this is why he applies this mystery to marriage.

Ephesians 5

> 21 *submitting yourselves one to another in the fear of God.*

This does not say that we are to blindly submit only to the apostles, prophets, evangelists, pastors, and teachers. Why? If we are submitted to the Lord, God can speak to us through any of our brethren that have the same commitment, be they male or female. The Lord may even use a child. How many times have we heard one of his little ones say something that maybe they did not even understand, and yet it pierced us to the core? And if we think that we are so important that we cannot listen to what is happening around us, we will not mature but will continue making a huge mistake because we do not have complete vision in and of ourselves.

The best we can do on our own (assuming that we can see and are not blind) is to see an arc of about 120 degrees or possibly 180 degrees with difficulty. To see the full 360 degrees requires two or three people at a time. This is why the Lord put us into a body. This is why there are other members of the body.

Scripture says that the most insignificant person – the smallest, the least, the servant of all – is the greatest in the kingdom of God. It is by the *nourishment that every connecting bond supplies, by the operation of each member according to measure they have received.* This is in the context of a marriage, *submitting yourselves one to another.*

Therefore the wife in this marriage should reflect and consider if God is trying to tell her something through her husband. There have been times when my wife gave advice based on her own flesh. To have followed this counsel would have been a disaster. But there have been other times when I was unable to see something but she could see it clearly. Because I did not submit to the anointing of the Lord that was flowing through her, damage occurred or time and effort were lost. We need a fine balance of discernment.

To know when we should listen to the serious input of our children or to tell them no, those things are not as they perceive them, requires the Spirit of God. This is part of the mystery of the will of God that he desires to reveal in us. This is a mystery that operates directly in our hearts but it also operates indirectly toward us through others who are pure in heart. Consider this layout:

> 22 *Wives, submit yourselves unto your own husbands, as unto the Lord.*

This is a two-way street because the husbands are not the Lord. They also must submit to the Lord. A woman who has a non-Christian husband must respect the position of that husband and know that the Lord has an office of authority there, but she must also submit to the Lord. Only the Lord can show her when she must submit to her husband and when she must only obey the higher authority which is the Lord. A woman who fears the Lord and is respectful of her unsaved husband may win him for Christ. This is according to Scripture.

> 23 *For the husband is the head of the wife even as the Christ is head of the congregation* {Gr. ekkle-sia – called out ones}, *and it is he who gives saving health to the body.*

Christ gives health to the body, but a natural family run by the woman is not so healthy. Many strong women are capable of great messages that sometimes have greater clarity in ministry than that of their husbands. These women have learned to maintain the proper respect and order regarding their husbands, and God has blessed and prospered them. I know strong women who are very wise in the Lord, for it is the faith of Jesus that operates in them. That is

He has placed these markers here in the Scripture like road signs to show us whether we are on the right track.

why this verse is not at the beginning of the letter, and we do not teach dry principles – do this, do that, submit here, etc. We do not select and attempt to operate in the flesh which will not work. We can only accomplish this by the Spirit.

This comes in the fifth chapter of the letter after speaking of the mystery of his will, what he desires to accomplish in our hearts, and where he wants to take us. He wants to not only take us out of darkness and bring us into the light, but he also wants us to be the light together with him in his inheritance. He has placed these markers here in the Scripture like road signs to show us whether we are on the right track. These are part of the good works that he has prepared for us to walk in.

Notice that he set the stage in advance:

Ephesians 5

1 *Be ye therefore imitators of God, as dear children*

2 *and walk in charity even as the Christ also has loved us and has given himself for us as an offering and a sacrifice to God for a sweet smelling savour.*

4 *neither dishonest words nor foolishness nor low jesting, which are not convenient, but rather giving of thanks.*

In the old covenant, the law went first, but the new covenant is backwards. In the new covenant, grace and faith go first, but they are not ours; they belong to him! Therefore, no one will glory in himself or herself. It is his grace and faith that must enter into us and give us this bond.

24 *Therefore, as the congregation* {Gr. ekklesia – called out ones} *is subject unto the Christ, so let the wives be to their own husbands in everything.*

25 *Husbands, love your wives even as the Christ also loved the congregation* {Gr. ekklesia – called out ones} *and gave himself for her,*

26 *that he might sanctify and cleanse her in the washing of water by the word,*

I have seen this operate in the natural realm – how a husband who is a conduit for the Lord and speaks the living Word of the Lord can cleanse his wife. When I met my wife, she saw something very different in me that she did not have. Her relationship with the Lord was through me, and when I was kidnapped and taken hostage for five months, she did not just lose her husband, she lost her priest, she lost her link with God. But God used the painful and traumatic persecution that we endured to establish a direct relationship with her. She had to live and experience the word that I had been preaching. This is what the Lord desires for all of his people.

It is very important that there is a clean word in this hour, and this can happen if there are pure hearts.

> 27 *that he might present her glorious for himself, a congregation* {Gr. ekklesia – called out ones}, *not having spot or wrinkle or any such thing, but that she should be holy and without blemish.*

Jude writes that *certain men crept in unawares without fear or reverence of God* and *These are the spots in your banquets of charity.* They do not have the same vision, and the Lord is calling to awaken and illuminate us so we can be the salt and the light. Those who do not heed these warnings will soon find themselves like the foolish virgins. They were virgins and had lamps, but they did not enter in because they ran out of oil. They were not connected to the source of the oil, the anointing which is him and only flows from his presence.

> 28 *So ought husbands to love their wives as their own bodies. He that loves his wife loves himself.*

> 29 *For no one ever hated his own flesh, but nourishes and cherishes it even as the Lord with his congregation* {Gr. ekklesia – called out ones}:

The husband who convinces his wife that he is willing to die for her will obtain her reverence. It will not be necessary to force her. The Lord does not force us; he invites us to come of our own free will. He does not have to convince us that he is willing to die. He already gave his life for all of us. So it is necessary to give him respect, reverence, and honor – what he deserves as our Head.

> 30 *For we are members of his body, of his flesh, and of his bones.*

31 *For this cause shall a man leave his father and mother and shall be joined unto his wife, and they shall be two in one flesh.*

32 *This is a great mystery, but I speak concerning Christ and the congregation* {Gr. ekklesia – called out ones}.

This is the same mystery as the mystery of the will of God. This is the same mystery as that of the head and the body coming together. This mystery cannot be understood except by revelation, by *the spirit of wisdom and revelation in the knowledge of him* (Ephesians 1:17). It is in the measure that we know him that wisdom and revelation will enter into us. It is his presence that transforms us.

In the old covenant, they had to kill sinners when the sin was too grievous.

In the old covenant, they had to kill sinners when the sin was too grievous. They had no other remedy. The law sentenced the adulterous woman to death (and the man also). It was a death sentence under a curse. But Jesus was able to say, *go and sin no more.* His word went forth with grace and power and everything she needed to be able to go forth trusting in him and not sin.

We must be careful to observe God's line of command described here. It goes from God to Christ to the husband to the wife to the children. If we spiritualize this and say that the children represent this and the wife represents that and the husband represents something else, what are we going to do with Christ and with God? This passage must be read as it is written, and any spiritual interpretation must be consistent.

Ephesians 6

1 *Children, obey your parents in the Lord, for this is right.*

Notice this does not say, "Children, blindly obey your parents no matter what." It is in the context of honoring our parents.

> 2 *Honour thy father and mother (which is the first commandment with a promise),*

> 3 *that it may be well with thee, and thou may live long on the earth.*

The commandment did not get canceled. The authority of the parents still exists, but under the new covenant, we are to obey them *in the Lord*. The Lord will show us if there is an exception – if something that our parents are telling us to do will pull us out of our bond with the Spirit. He will show us how to continue to honor our parents even if there are times when they become difficult and impossible.

This is a fine balance that only a person under the control of the Holy Spirit can manage. This is part of the mystery of the will of God. He does not remove us from the realm of the powers that be. He does not remove us from our natural family. He does not tell us that those of the world are no longer important now that we are walking with Christ. No, according to Scripture, we are to walk circumspectly in such a way as to convince them of the truth.

And it may be possible to convince them if the Holy Spirit is moving us. Even if we make a mistake and fail, it is still possible to redeem the time with real and authentic repentance.

> 4 *And, ye fathers, provoke not your children to wrath, but bring them up in the discipline and admonition of the Lord.*

> 5 *Slaves, be obedient to those that are your masters according to the flesh, with fear and trembling, in simplicity of your heart as unto the Christ,*

He does not tear down the lines of human authority. He does, however, cause them to work in a different manner.

A man who had been in the service of the Devil since childhood and lived a life of unspeakable atrocities, including a serious sexual problem, surrendered to the Lord, was baptized in water, and was touched by the Holy Spirit. This happened after he had listened to us on the radio for quite a while. He understood the covenant he was making with the Lord. We explained that the Lord would become directly involved in his life to train and discipline him. He was fine with this.

Two days later, I got an urgent phone call. He said he was gravely ill and needed help to get to the hospital. He claimed to be having heart problems and said he was unable to get out of bed. I detected a strong sense of self-pity in his voice. When we heard the rest of the story, we learned that his old friends had come by and convinced him to go out for another night on the town. As they crossed the first street corner, they met some policemen. One of them insulted the policemen who then lit into them with their billy clubs and beat them black and blue from head to foot. The old "friends" split up and ran away. Somehow this fellow managed to get back across the street and into his apartment. And then he could not figure out why things were going so bad for him right after he had come to the Lord!

The only thing I had to do was to explain that the Lord had begun to work on his life. He had sent all those nice policemen to effect some correction and discipline. The guy broke into tears and said, "I can't take any more of this. I don't want the Lord to intervene if it is going to be like this."

I told him, "Too late! It is not easy to enter into a covenant with the Lord, and after he has taken you on, it will not be easy to get out of it." Years have gone by, and every time this fellow gets into trouble, the Lord brings it to light and nails him. We have seen him receive some very serious dealings which are the consequences of his previous behavior. In and through it all, he realizes that God has been extremely merciful to him, and he has not received what he really deserved. God left him crippled and limping, but he is walking as best he can in the right direction.

This is by the power of God, by the grace of God. It is only with Christ inside of us that this works. Obviously, the more docile we are the easier it is.

> 10 *Finally, my brethren, be strong in the Lord and in the power of his might.*

This is power under control. When power is not under control, it is violent. God always uses his power under control. When his power is in us, it must be under the control of the Spirit of God. The Lord gives us gifts for this purpose and observes us to see what we do with them. If we are born with a gift in the area of music and use our gift in an evil way in a bar or somewhere else, God does not immediately withdraw the gift. He allows us to continue until the time of the harvest. The same holds true in the spiritual realm. Therefore,

> 11 *Put on the whole armour of God that ye may be able to stand firm against the wiles of the devil.*

> 12 *For we wrestle not against flesh and blood, but against principalities, against powers, against the lords of this age, rulers of this darkness, against spiritual wickedness in the heavens.*

> 13 *Therefore, take unto you the whole armour of God, that ye may be able to withstand in the evil day and stand fast, all the work having been finished.*

Having finished what work? The work of God – the work that he ordained in advance for us to walk in, the work of Christ.

Our salvation is by grace and by faith, but the final judgment is by works. *Ye shall know them by their fruits.* This is not referring to our works. It is referring to his works that he has done in and through us. If righteousness has come forth in us, it is his work. This is the only way to tell the wheat from the tares.

> 14 *Stand firm, therefore, having your loins girt about with truth and having on the breastplate,* {the coat of mail and coat of arms} *of righteousness,*

The Lord Jesus is the truth. He is the covering for our spiritual nakedness. The *breastplate of righteousness* is mistranslated. It really refers to a seamless coat of chain mail that protects the person from the neck to their ankles. There are no chinks in this armor. The righteousness of God is total protection.

In the Old Testament there were two kings who took off their kingly seamless armor and disguised themselves with inferior armor because they were afraid to be singled out as the king. Both were shot and killed on separate occasions when an arrow pierced the leather juncture along the sides (1 Kings 22:30-34; 2 Chronicles 35:22-23).

This is what happens when we make our decisions based on the fear of man. The love of God (charity) casts out fear. If we react to the fear of man, we may be shot by the enemy further down the road. These kings were afraid to be identified as the kings of Israel and of Judah. God wants us to be identified as sons of God and as nothing else.

> 15 *and your feet shod with the preparation of the gospel of peace,*

Moses had to take off his sandals at the burning bush when he stood on the holy ground of God's purposes. His education and training at Pharaoh's house were no good to him as God sent him to deliver Israel. We are to be shod with the preparations God has made in us as we have walked with him. Man's preparation and training will not work. Only the presence of God prepares us; being with Jesus prepared Peter and John and the others.

In the Song of Solomon when the bride is in the final stages of preparation, Scripture says, *How beautiful are thy feet in thy shoes, O prince's daughter!* – indicating that she is now royalty and prepared to represent him as he is. This is another part of the mystery of this marriage.

> *Anyone who attacks her gets into the same trouble as if they were attacking him.*

It is Christ in us that is the hope of glory. Anyone who attacks her gets into the same trouble as if they were attacking him.

Revelation 11

4 *These are the two olive trees and the two lampstands standing before the God of the earth.*

5 *And if anyone desires to hurt them, fire proceeds out of their mouth and devours their enemies; and if anyone desires to hurt them, he must in this manner be killed.*

God's judgments are not arbitrary. He allows judgment to come forth from every heart. What these enemies desire to do to the Lord and to his people is exactly what is likely to happen to them.

Ephesians 6

16 *above all, taking the shield of faith, with which ye shall be able to quench all the fiery darts of the wicked.*

We must take hold of the shield, which is our job, but the shield belongs to him. His faith operates in us by the Spirit to snuff out all the fiery darts of the enemy, not just block them.

With his shield, we can put out all the false fire of the enemy so that only the true fire of God remains. The church does not know this realm of victory. There is much false fire among those who claim to represent God today. People do things that they claim are manifestations of the Spirit of God, but they are not because they do not have the faith of Christ to quench all those fiery darts of the enemy.

When God is doing something, the enemy likes to attempt the same thing. This happened when Moses went down to see Pharaoh, whose magicians attempted to duplicate what God was doing through Moses. False prophets and false apostles continue to do the same today.

> 17 *And take the helmet of salvation and the sword of the Spirit, which is the word of God;*

Please note that this armor is not made of common things that are lying around. All of it is connected to him. The sword relates to him, as do the helmet and the shield. The footgear is established so he can order our steps and send us, such that our steps please him. We must put off the old man and put on the new man, which is Christ (Ephesians 4:22-24). He is the only one who can overcome all our adversaries. He is the overcomer. In the Old Testament, most of the psalms were dedicated to the "overcomer" (Christ), but over time and with usage, the word got interpreted as the "choir director."

How can we put on this armor and keep it on?

> 18 *praying always with all prayer and supplication in the Spirit and watching in this with all persever- ance and supplication for all the saints.*

There are several words translated "prayer" in the New Testament. This is not the word for petitionary prayer or for emergency help. This word means an ongoing, unbroken rela- tionship with the Father. This is not a religious exercise, but an unbroken bond of fellowship with God. This is the word that Jesus used when he told the disciples that *this lineage of demons does not go out but by prayer and fasting* (Matthew 17:14-21).

Jesus did not stop his ministry to take out a few hours, days, or weeks for prayer and fasting. No, he instantly cast out the demon. He lived 24/7 in an unbroken bond of fellowship with his Father, and he was always "fasting" in that he never fed his own ego. He was always

> *He lived 24/7 in an unbroken bond of fellowship with his Father*

doing the will of his Father (Isaiah 58). The Father showed him in an instant what to do, and the demon had no choice but to flee. Not only has the church not been able to handle this lineage of demons and to advance, but the enemy has invaded and is now inside. Church people are fleeing everywhere when God tells us how to *withstand in the evil day and stand fast, all the work having been finished.*

This topic of the mysteries of God is very extensive.

Revelation 10

> *7 but in the day of the voice of the seventh angel when he shall begin to sound the trumpet, the mystery of God shall be finished, as he did evangelize unto his slaves the prophets.*

I believe that we are very close to the day of these trumpets. The trumpets of God are the message of God's way – when God himself speaks through a people with pure hearts. This mystery will be fulfilled and will be seen. The Lord Jesus will return for a bride without spot or wrinkle or any such thing, but this is impossible for man. For this reason, many do not really believe in this.

They believe that Jesus will come to rapture a bride that is sick and crippled and stained and defeated. This is not what will happen. He will have a bride that is pure and undefiled.

He will have a people who will represent him as he is, and the world will have the opportunity to receive or reject a clean, authentic, and true expression of who he is.

Let us pray:

Heavenly Father, we thank you for beginning to reveal unto us the mystery of your will, the mystery of the gospel. We ask that this mystery may be revealed and put into effect in the heart of each of us. We ask this in the name of our Lord Jesus Christ. Amen.

CHAPTER 8

Open Doors in the Heavens

As we look at Psalm 30, we recognize that *thirty* implies maturity. This same word in Greek and Hebrew also means "perfection." It is interesting that on January 3, 2014, it had been thirty years since I was released from my first kidnapping. We have spent the past thirty years in a different kind of ministry. Before this, I was managing a farm, flying airplanes as a bush pilot in the jungle, and caring for cows. I built wood-framed houses and managed a large, walk-in freezer for fish. But all of this changed.

There was a time of transition that lasted about 150 days – just like in Revelation chapter 9 when the locusts were let loose, and they stung men like scorpions. I learned something about scorpions in the jungle. They are not snakes. They don't kill you. But you know what? You will never forget the sting of a scorpion. Never. You can forget about any other kind of bite like that of a bee or a wasp, but you can't forget the sting of a scorpion.

When I found myself kidnapped, I was twenty-seven years old. I had worked hard, and I was almost overwhelmed by the "sting" of the scorpion. Why? Even though I hoped that I would get out of there alive, I knew I wouldn't have any money afterward. All my money and possessions completely vanished.

This sting was painful and hard. God says that the entire world is going to experience a time like this.

Many have already suffered this throughout the centuries since John wrote Revelation. But before the end, the entire world will be stung by this scorpion. The people who think they are Christians while they are still lukewarm will go through this before the coming of the Lord. But the promise also comes in the same text because God prohibits those same locusts that sting like scorpions from touching any green thing.

our hope is not in the things of this world.

Green represents the life of God, of Christ in us. Even if it is just a few green leaves that are sprouting, the locusts cannot touch it. And our hope is not in the things of this world. If we do not invest the things of this world into the kingdom of God, they will be lost completely. Ever since the time of my captivity, my heart has not been inclined to store up the things of this world. (This is a clear message in the book of the Acts of the Apostles.)

My heart's desire has been to invest in the kingdom of God and his righteousness. This means having a heart for other people. What is not invested under the guidance of the Holy Spirit will be lost. But the investment we have made for the kingdom of God will have eternal results. And the most important thing that we can invest in the kingdom of God is not even our money, although we can invest that. I am convinced that it is not our money; it is our time. It is possible to acquire more money, but it is impossible to acquire more time.

Psalm 30

A Psalm and Song at the dedication of the house of David.

And we know that in a greater and more sublime sense, the house of David is nothing less than the body of Christ which will soon come to maturity and receive the fullness of the inheritance.

> 1 *I will extol thee, O LORD; for thou hast lifted me up and hast not made my foes to rejoice over me.*

You remember the story. David told the Lord that he wanted to build him a house. And do you remember the response that the Lord gave David? The Lord told David, "No, you will not build my house. I am going to build your house, and in your lineage your heir will be the Messiah [the Christ]."

God told David that there was too much blood stained on his hands. He said, "You have been in too many battles and wars. I will raise up your son Solomon, and he will be a son of peace." Solomon means "peace offering."

> 2 *O LORD my God, I cried unto thee, and thou hast healed me.*

> 3 *O LORD, thou hast brought up my soul from Sheol; thou gavest me life from my descent into the grave.*

> 4 *Let his merciful ones sing unto the LORD, and give thanks at the remembrance of his holiness.*

> 5 *For his anger endures but a moment; in his will is life; weeping may endure for a night, but joy comes in the morning.*

We have all come through times of weeping during the night. If we are true sons of God, we have endured many tests. We have been in many circumstances where we know without a shadow of a doubt that there is no way out unless there is a miracle, unless God intervenes directly in our situation. It has happened to me many times. And there are still circumstances and situations that continue to happen like this.

> *And hast not made my foes to rejoice over me.*

The Lord has done the same with me. My enemies have not been able to rejoice over me. And when they began to rejoice over me, God himself intervened with a great force. And I think, "Who am I that the Lord would intervene in this way?"

Like David, I've thought that maybe I am not that good or very important, but for some reason the Lord made the determination that my enemies are not going to mock me. My enemies are not going to say, "We told you so; we said all along that he was going to come to a bad end."

Above and beyond all the possibilities and predictions, here we stand by the mercy of God. The adventures have been many and long, and they even continue. But here we are. This year and every year for me begins on the third of January. It was on the third of January 1964, that our family arrived in Colombia (for the first time) as missionaries. We have now completed fifty years of family ministry, and our fiftieth anniversary was held on January 3, 2014.

Twenty years after our arrival in Colombia, I was released from the first kidnapping on the exact same date and to the hour! Last year, as we had our forty-ninth anniversary, and as we began our fiftieth year, which was our "Year of Jubilee," guess where I was? I was seated on an airliner with a first-class ticket (except that I gave my seat to Albert) on my way to Havana. I sat in the back with Doctor Fernando in the midst of another adventure that included much opposition. Albert (who was eighty-eight years old) prayed for some key people, and God healed all of them. Some possibilities opened up. These possibilities resulted in us making a total of seven trips – seven secret but blessed trips. But I cannot say any more about this at this time.

We are literally on the edge of our seats as we have great expectations about what God will do in the coming months and years. It will be interesting. We came to Colombia as a family in 1964, and on May 27, the war was formalized in Colombia. We do not claim to know all the details about God's plans, but we do know that he has his hand on us and on Colombia. I do not believe that it is the will of God for this war to continue for more than fifty years.

6 *And in my prosperity I said, I shall never be moved.*

God has prospered us in fifty years of ministry starting with my wife, my children, and my extended spiritual family, and which includes many of you and many others as well. In the gospel of Mark, God makes a promise:

Mark 10

29 *Jesus said, Verily I say unto you, There is no one that has left house or brethren or sisters or father or mother or wife or children or lands for my sake and the gospel's*

30 *who shall not receive one hundredfold now in this time: houses and brethren and sisters and mothers and children and lands, with persecutions, and in the world to come eternal life.*

In my case we may have received more than one hundredfold. You cannot imagine how many houses are open to us where we are treated as family. I have a lot of keys in my drawers because many people have given us the keys to their houses and I cannot fit them onto a key chain. The Lord has prospered us.

Psalm 30

6 *And in my prosperity I said, I shall never be moved.*

David did not take the kingdom away from Saul by violence. He did not stretch forth his hand even in the midst of much injustice. David received his prosperity directly from God. He was thirty-seven years old when he received the fullness of the kingdom, and then he began to build his house. The Lord gave him victory over all his enemies and over all the enemies of the people of God. Not even one enemy had the strength to remain standing.

> 7 LORD, by thy favour thou hast made my mountain to stand strong.

This is the mountain of David, of Sion, of God. Scripture speaks of another mountain, the mountain of religiosity. The Lord mentioned this after he cursed the fig tree which is a figure representing the religiosity of man when man desires to use God instead of being used by God.

Mark 11

> 23 For verily I say unto you that whosoever shall say unto this mountain, Remove thyself and cast thyself into the sea, and shall not doubt in his heart but shall believe that what he says shall be done whatsoever he says shall be done unto him.

As Jesus, Peter, James, and John were coming down off the Mount of Transfiguration, they encountered a multitude, and in the midst of the crowd was the man with the demon-possessed son whom Jesus' disciples had been unable to cure.

Matthew 17

> 18 And Jesus rebuked him, and the demon departed out of him and the child was cured from that very hour.

> 19 Then the disciples came to Jesus apart and said, Why could not we cast him out?

> 20 And Jesus said unto them, Because of your unfaithfulness; for verily I say unto you, If ye have faith as a grain of mustard seed, ye shall say to this mountain,

Remove from here to yonder place, and it shall
remove; and nothing shall be impossible unto you.

David removed the mountain of falseness, oppression, and false religiosity that has no real power. He removed this mountain that robs the sons of God of their inheritance. David overcame this mountain in the name of the Lord. It was cast down and remained so to the end of David's life and then some. Yet this is only a type and shadow of the reality that we are about to live!

It had become popular to
level false charges against me.

Psalm 30

7 *LORD, by thy favour thou hast made my mountain to stand strong; thou didst hide thy face, and I was troubled.*

8 *I will cry unto thee, O GOD; and unto the Lord will I make supplication.*

9 *What profit is there in my blood when I go down to the pit? Shall the dust praise thee? Shall it declare thy truth?*

The Lord has not allowed me to go down to the dust of the pit or to jail even though, like David, we have had many difficult moments. There was a dangerous criminal in jail attempting to blackmail me for a lot of money – threatening to falsely accuse me if I did not come up with the money. And he was not the first. It had become popular to level false charges against me. It seemed almost for sure that if they were not able to kill me, I would at least spend many years in prison in a country that has no bail. No one knows the future except for the Lord. But do you know what? Here I am. And I have not had to defend myself. Is that not interesting?

Most of those with the railing accusations against us are gone. They have their own problems. Some have been transferred or fired. Those who have placed a price on my head have gone from bad to worse. Some of them are limping around or lying in bed dying even as they continue to rail against my friends and me. They are hiding out in some jungle and cannot get up. They cannot see the light of day, and we can go anywhere the Lord sends us.

> 10 *Hear, O LORD and have mercy upon me: LORD, be thou my helper.*
>
> 11 *Thou hast turned my mourning into dancing: thou hast put off my sackcloth and girded me with gladness;*
>
> 12 *to the end that I may sing glory unto thee and not be silent. O LORD my God, I will give thanks unto thee for ever.*

This is a short psalm of only twelve verses. Twelve is the number of divine order, of the government of God. This is where David found the key to perfection and maturity. I see something unique about God – he does not multiply anything that does not meet his standards. If there is no maturity or perfection, he will not multiply it. Until now God has been adding (what would turn out later to be very important) people one by one. We have been running around in the wilderness like King David. We have been so persecuted that sometimes we have even had to seek refuge among the "Philistines." I have gotten up in the morning and felt like King David who all of a sudden found himself marching in the Philistine army to fight against Israel (1 Samuel 28:1, 2; 29:2). How did the roles get reversed? But God delivered David from this also.

David wrote that it was Saul's fault he had to seek refuge

with the Philistines. In the midst of so many enemies, in the midst of such wickedness, in the midst of so many adversaries, we have been surrounded and faced with every type of corrupt people on all sides (including repeated head-on encounters with terrorists, mafia, and corrupt officials over the past thirty years) and not just from Colombia. They have singled us out for attack from incredible places.

In the midst of this, do you know who have been our worst enemies? Who have been the most hidden, most serious, most unreliable, most dangerous, and most like Judas? It is the false religious people. It is those who have the whitewashed exterior but are corrupt inside. They throw stones and hide their hand. They aim the arrow and have someone else shoot it. They smile and greet us with a hug, but their smile is superficial and with their hug comes a knife in our back.

But, you know what? Here we are, standing tall. And we will be here, standing firm and tall as long as the Lord decrees. If we are not detained, we will continue to go wherever the Lord sends us.

If we are killed, do you know what will happen? The Lord will multiply things even quicker because this is how he works. It is when we die that God can multiply us; therefore, the apostle Paul could say, *For to me to live is Christ and to die is gain.* I am convinced that we are entering into a new stage in which the blessing of God will be measured by a different standard. We have been walking under many shadows of death thinking, where is the exit? yet knowing that only the Lord can get us out of this. In the times of greatest darkness, in the most difficult moments, do you know what the Lord has done? He has not taken us out of the problems. He ordered the blessing to overtake us from behind!

We are not seeking things. Yet the Lord overtook us with his blessing from behind, and it is increasing. The enemies that appeared to be giants are seeking to hide. They do not know what to do. The true blessing, as the Shulamite discovered, is not things; it is not even opportunities. The true blessing is the presence of the Lord, and this presence begins small, hidden in our hearts. But the Lord is capable of making his presence in us shine so it can be seen from far away. The enemies are not afraid of us; they are afraid of the Lord. The demons are having problems – lots of problems.

The enemies are not afraid of us; they are afraid of the Lord.

The fiftieth year was the Year of Jubilee when everything was returned to its proper owner. Who is the real owner? It is the Lord. The beginning of the year 2017, which on the Jewish calendar begins on the first day of the seventh month (September or October of 2016, if I have added and subtracted accurately), will be the beginning of the seventieth Year of Jubilee since the exodus of the people of Israel from Egypt when they left Mount Sinai and headed towards the Promised Land.

The sixty-ninth Jubilee, which was fulfilled in 1967, brought great blessings: the Six-Day War in Israel, and the charismatic movement in Colombia with the earthquake of February 9, 1967, which shook every single cathedral in Colombia. That year many ministries flourished, like the ministry of Richard Wurmbrand when he was freed. The colleges and universities of the United States overflowed with hippies and protestors of the Vietnam War. God profoundly touched many of them until they were called the Jesus People. Many, many ministries came forth. That was the sixty-ninth Jubilee. What may God have in store for the seventieth?

About thirty years ago, I was sitting in the jungles of the lower Guaviare River in eastern Colombia. I felt that I was the only missionary left after hundreds had fled. I remember thinking, *Surely the Lord has a great reward in store for me, surely the Lord will bless me in an extraordinary manner. I know that God has good intentions concerning me.* I was thinking like this when – Bam! They kidnapped me! I spent five months tied to a tree in the jungle. That experience changed the course of my life.

Manuel Marulanda Vélez (alias Tirofijo, the founder of the Colombian FARC guerrilla movement) had chosen his best young people for a special forces course to train them to be top leaders. In order to graduate, he gave them a very difficult task: they had to kidnap a Gringo (an American). This turned into a no-brainer since most of the other Gringos had left, and I was about the only one left. But when I left the guerrilla camp, I was friends with all of them. I left with the authorization of Don Manuel and he was famous for keeping his word. He said that my brother and I could remain and live among them wherever they had control, and he kept that word until the day he died. This gave a very different opportunity to present the gospel than typically used by religion and religious people.

We have been involved in a work not centering in meetings, even though we have had some meetings. This endeavor does not have its center in rites or rituals, nor even in superficial experiences. We are not trying to see how many people we can water baptize or how many people can take communion or how many can be convinced to tithe.

It is possible that all these things have had their place in history as in the times of King David when the Israelites sacrificed lambs and bullocks and doves. Even though all this was written in the Law, the Lord changed everything and started a new period of history. Yet residual teachings of that Jewish religiosity infiltrated (even leavened) the church and have been fermenting for almost two thousand years.

Many sincere people have followed these practices and customs, and I am not completely against that which has had its proper time and place. I am simply saying that we are entering a new day in God where these practices are not the reality. Reality is to walk 24/7 with the Lord even if they cast us out of religious encampments. It is better to be outside the camp where there is less contamination. The apostle Paul wrote something that seemed absurd, and surely it was the beginning of what cost him his life later on:

1 Corinthians 1

17 For Christ sent me not to baptize, but to preach the gospel.

He mentioned two or three that he had baptized before he received that clarity, and maybe he baptized some more afterward. He left the meeting at the first council of Jerusalem after prevailing with the apostles and elders. Everyone accepted that it was not necessary to circumcise the Gentile believers (Acts 15), but Paul straightway circumcised Timothy (Acts 16:3).

Why did he do this? The apostles and elders had all accepted that it seemed good to them and to the Holy Spirit to not circumcise. So why did he circumcise Timothy? It was Paul's policy to preach to the Jews first and then to the Gentiles. They were headed to Corinth, and Crispus, the prince of the synagogue of Corinth, would become converted (Acts 18:8-11). This meant that the Christians did not get kicked out of the synagogue at Corinth as in most other places.

So, Paul ministered inside a Jewish synagogue in Corinth for a year and six months (similar to the situation in Jerusalem), and Timothy helped him as his companion in ministry. Paul could not take Timothy into the synagogue without circumcising him first. Their first priority was to join the people to Christ, not to attack the religious rites and rituals that many were clinging to. These things would come down under their own weight at the proper time. Jesus said that he did not come to do away with the Law and the prophets; he came to fulfill them. He did this with his own sacrifice, and that did away with animal sacrifice forever.

So Paul wrote to Timothy and Titus who were helping him at Corinth to be careful with Jewish law and tradition. He said the women were to remain silent according to the law of the Jews, but to the new Christians who were congregating in other places, he wrote that in Christ there is neither Jew nor Gentile; in Christ there is neither slave nor free; in Christ there is neither male nor female. He even dared to write that whosoever is led by the Spirit is not under the law (Galatians 3:28; 5:18).

When the Holy Spirit leads us to smuggle Bibles into countries with a government that is hostile to Christianity or to beam clandestine radio broadcasts into satanic enemy strongholds we do not have to obey the law. However, those who break the law (even for seemingly pious purposes) when they are not being explicitly led by the Spirit could very likely come to a disastrous end.

To those of the Jewish synagogue in Corinth, Paul wrote:

1 Corinthians 9

19 Therefore, though I am free regarding everyone, yet I have made myself slave unto all, that I might gain the more.

20 And unto the Jews I became as a Jew, that I might gain the Jews; to those who are under the law, as under the law, that I might gain those that are under the law;

21 to those that are without law, as without law (being not without law of God, but under the law of Christ), that I might gain those that are without law.

Under the Jews, in order to enter into a covenant with God (the old covenant), the sign of the covenant was circumcision of the flesh. This meant that only the men could enter into covenant with God because it is impossible to circumcise a woman. She had to remain silent in the synagogue and listen to her husband.

Under the new covenant, however, the Holy Spirit effects circumcision in the heart so men, women, and children can enter into a direct covenant and have direct contact with God. If the person has a pure heart and is in direct contact with God by the Holy Spirit, and God has cleansed them and is using them, who are we to say no?

I am with Paul. The Lord has not sent me to baptize, but if I jog my memory, I think I have baptized a few. There can still be some good reasons for baptizing in specific cases, such as when someone must minister back in the religious "synagogues" which are all over town. They will not receive us in most of those churches unless we have been baptized in water.

Another complicating factor in Colombia and all over the Caribbean is that the dominating religion is not Roman Catholicism. Rather, it is "Santeria" or spiritualism in which the shamans mix worshipping the "saints" with occult practices imported from Africa and elsewhere. These saints include the late Hugo Chavez of Venezuela and many others. In order to participate in the rites and rituals of Santeria, the people must first be water baptized in any Christian church. This is a diabolical plot to mix Christians with witchcraft. In some Caribbean nations, all church buildings belong to the state, and pictures of those who are to be worshipped are in prominent display inside the sanctuaries.

For those who are receiving the Lord in the mountains or jungles or even in the cities, if they are not called by God to penetrate those places of serious spiritual corruption, I believe that baptism in water can be dangerous. I have a witness from the Holy Spirit to leave the people incompatible with that system.

I used to think that there are three baptisms, but I was wrong. I thought there was baptism in water, baptism in the Holy Spirit, and baptism in fire. However, in Ephesians 4:5 it says there is *one Lord, one faith, and one baptism.*

The real baptism is the one that only the Lord Jesus can accomplish (immersion into his name or nature by the Holy Spirit). His real baptism is impossible to falsify (it produces the real fruit of the Spirit). The water baptism that we can accomplish is a symbol (a type or a shadow) of the real thing, but it is easy for corruption to occur and for unclean spirits to be transferred to new depths if the practice of water baptism is presided over by corrupt ministers of a false gospel.

The water baptism that we can accomplish is a symbol of the real thing

John the Baptist said: *I indeed baptize you in water unto repentance, but he that comes after me is mightier than I, whose shoes I am not worthy to bear; he shall baptize you in* [Gr. into] *the Holy Spirit and fire* (Matthew 3:11).

The baptism into *the Holy Spirit and fire* is one baptism because Jesus immerses us into the fire of his dealings by the Holy Spirit. Water is a symbol in the ritual washing of the Jews prescribed by the Law. Water baptism is a very explicit symbol: we must die to the past and rise out of the water to a new life in the Lord. All of this is very beautiful, but if the Lord Jesus is not baptizing us into the Holy Spirit and fire, which only he can do, and we continue only with water baptisms, the people will only come out of the water wet! Or worse yet, they can be tainted with the unclean religious spirit of a corrupt minister.

This is like the fable of *The Emperor's New Clothes*. They came and told him they were going to make him some fine and costly clothes with gold thread and diamonds. Everyone admired all the details of the con job because no one wanted to admit to being a fool. The money was stolen, and the emperor was running around naked until a child blurted out the truth!

Without the real baptism in the Holy Spirit and fire, which can only be accomplished by the Lord, we do not have anything. If we do not enter in to do good works by the Holy Spirit, we have no covering (Revelation 19:8). The covering is not submission to a human ministry that apparently has gifts and a lot of talent. No sir! Our covering is to do the will of God. If we are to be faithful ministers of the Lord, we all must have the Holy Spirit, and we are all to minister (serve).

Our task is to join others to the Lord and let the Lord handle them. We are not to stir up the pot. We are not to do things that God is not doing. The Lord is doing things, and he is doing them with what looks like the least-likely people. Somewhere, somehow, under certain circumstances, God puts them under conviction. Some have received a radio. Others have received a Bible. Others simply were out in the jungle, and God touched them directly. Many have had family or friends praying for them for years.

One of the last persons healed here in Bogotá who had a deformed foot was told by Albert to take off her sock and shoe and put her foot up on the coffee table in our living room while he called everyone to gather around and pray. But before any of us could pray, God healed the foot as everyone was watching! We were not even ready to pray, and the deformed foot straightened right out. Is it not better if the Lord receives all the credit and all the glory?

It would be sad if in the midst of the blessing that God is about to pour out and is pouring out, there would be people worshipping us. This would be very sad, would it not?

If the country opens up, and people can walk through the mountains and jungles with tranquility, what will we find? Incredible testimonies are waiting to be discovered – stories of what God has been doing in the most-forgotten corners. It is not essential to study courses of theology in order to be used by the Lord.

Do you remember the Samaritan woman in the gospel of John? She was at the well. She did not disappear for years and get a degree. She spent about five minutes with the Lord and then went out and evangelized the town. The majority of the people were converted. I read that there were little towns and places like hers where there has been an unbroken thread of Christians throughout the violent history that took place on all sides when Jerusalem was repeatedly destroyed into ruins upon ruins. In these little places, Christians who were not even from a Jewish background survived all the devastation that went on around them for centuries. They received the Lord, and history treated them differently. They literally received the Lord as he came walking by when the religious people would not. When the Lord sent out his disciples, the people had to receive the people that the Lord sent. The Lord is sending again. He is sending us (Matthew 10:40-42).

The most important thing is not to put everyone down on their knees to repeat prayers and to participate in religious ritual. If they know who we are, if they know that the Lord sent us, and if they receive us, they receive Jesus. And if they receive the Lord Jesus, they receive the Father (John 13:20). There is no more need for religious ritual. If the Lord enters and circumcises their hearts and baptizes them into the Holy Spirit and immerses them into his own nature, what more could we do?

It is time to cut with superficial religiosity. Who are any of us to claim that the tithes of the Lord belong to us or to our organization? It is much better to let the Lord move on every heart. The new covenant is not a tithe; it is a willingness to let the Lord manage all of our being – not only our money but also our time. If we have ill-gotten gains, it is better to let them go even if this is uncomfortable.

Someone came under conviction to consult one of the great pastors of this city because he had been involved in the theft of a large sum of money from the government by corrupt politicians. He came to confess this to the pastor, but the earthly-minded pastor's reply was, "And have you paid your tithe on this?"

> *The Lord may not give the same message to everyone.*

The Lord may not give the same message to everyone. What he said to the rich young ruler was not exactly the same as what he said to others. The Lord knows where our heart is, and the person who has the god of money reigning in his heart will have to let go of that god to truly follow the Lord.

A good friend of ours felt that the Lord told him to get rid of the TV set in his house, and he did. His family was very upset about this, but he did it. The real problem occurred after he got rid of his TV set. He felt called to a new ministry – the ministry of getting rid of everyone else's TV sets. We have a problem if the Lord does not tell the neighbor to give up his TV set. So, guilt trips are laid on those who resist. A terrible, gooey religiosity began to develop, and he managed to make us feel a bit guilty about this and about many other things. About this time, we were caring for another missionary's house while they were on furlough. We had looked for a place to stay, and they left us their house, completely furnished, dog included. Almost every room had a TV set.

Our entire family seemed happy watching TV. All the TVs were connected to cable, and there was a lot of diversity. This was all quite novel for us twenty-five years ago in Bogotá. I saw that some of the programs were a bit intense but since the Lord had provided the place for us, maybe he wanted to teach each family member about discernment. The only thing that really bothered me was the big TV in the master bedroom which my wife, Marina, loved to watch (she says I was watching it too).

I decided to have a talk with her about removing the TV from our bedroom. I had to turn off the TV in the middle of a program, and this made it so that she was not in the best disposition. So she said, "Well, why don't you let the Lord show us if we should remove this TV or not?" Boom! A bolt of lightning hit the house. Even though the TV was turned off, the screen became white and then red-hot as the TV blew up in our faces. We went without a TV in our room until the owners of the house returned, and we had to pay for the damages.

So our children grew up, and I never bought TV sets. But TVs would show up at our house like magic, and the boys ended up having a little Sony TV. One day they came in to see me and said, "Dad, we want to buy a complete home theater for our house with 5.1 surround sound and a giant screen."

I said, "I don't think so." I told them that we were behind in a lot of things concerning the ministry, and we had many needs. I could not justify the expense. I told them there was no way we could do it.

So, a few weeks went by. Russ Jr. and Dylan came back and said, "God has put it in our hearts to have another talk with you about the home theater we want to buy. God put it in our hearts to ask, 'How much money does the ministry need this month?'"

So I added up all the normal expenses. Then I added up the expense of all the special problems that needed to be solved. There were a few bills that had to be paid off. Then I added something for unexpected needs that might occur and rounded it all off to a nice sum. I told them that the ministry needed fifty thousand dollars.

They replied, "It is good for us to know all this, Dad, so we are going to pray for fifty-one thousand two hundred dollars to come in this month – fifty thousand for the ministry and twelve hundred for our home theater. We are going to come back in a month, and you are going to tell us how much money came in."

The month went by, and the two of them came back to talk about this right on schedule. I got out the accounts and bank ledgers and went over all kinds of complicated receipts with dollars and cents that had come in from many different directions. Unbelievably, it all added up to exactly fifty thousand dollars. I was overjoyed that the Lord had sent such marvelous provision for the ministry, but their faces fell. However, as we were leaving our house in Bogotá to go somewhere, we found two envelopes in the mailbox from the government of the United States. President Obama had just been elected and had sent every adult American taxpayer a stimulus check for six hundred dollars. There was one for me and one for Marina: twelve hundred dollars.

So, I didn't have to pay for the home theater, nor did we use any money from the ministry. Obama did it! This was the beginning of God accelerating a desire in the hearts of our children and young people to make a movie. He kept adding equipment and details until they were able to film a full feature movie designed to be released in theaters, which has been a great blessing to the ministry. Every detail, every line, every piece of equipment was ordered and orchestrated by the Lord.

My daughters, Lisa and Alethia, spent years writing the script and directing and producing the movie *La Montaña*. Hundreds of actors, extras, and a production crew donated their time to make this project a success. Several times, well-meaning people have attempted to change the movie, and I have had to defend the young people who made it.

The impact of the film on Colombia has been amazing. We thought that the target audience would be the uncouth soldiers, paramilitaries, guerrillas, and campesinos depicted in the movie. We thought that church people would not accept the rough language of the reality portrayed, but we are continually amazed. Hundreds of pastors have been brought to profound repentance watching that movie. The Holy Spirit convicted them of fighting over doctrine, sheep, and finances within the confines of their little religious fortresses instead of seeking the lost sheep in the highways and byways. Many have said that the Lord showed them they must stop what they are doing and start over.

Recently, we had another family meeting and came to the conclusion that we are now standing in front of the widest open doors for ministry that we have ever seen in the history of this country. We have the possibility at this moment of being able to reach into all the seemingly impossible corners of this country and do things that we could have never imagined. We have friends on all sides, and all our friends are also in the fire of persecution while the Lord continues to prosper them.

Marina and I thought, *Who is going to pray? Let's pray for an amount, for the resources to take advantage of all the wonderful opportunities.* But none of our young people dared to pray for a specific amount. The reality is that we do not know what or how much will be needed. And as we do not know, we don't know if we need a million dollars or five million. We don't know all the plans that the Lord may have for Colombia, so it is better if we do not name an amount. Because, you know what? If the Lord really opens the doors of heaven, he will supply everything that is needed.

There are doors open here on earth as never before. But, brethren, we need open doors in the heavens. The open doors in the heavens happen when there are men and women and children willing to do the will of God without considering the consequences and without considering their own lives.

Let us pray:

Heavenly Father, we ask for open doors in the heavens. We ask that we may remain focused and not waver, that we may first seek the kingdom of God and your righteousness. May we rest everything else in your hands. We ask this in the name of our Lord Jesus Christ. Amen.

About the Author

Russell Stendal, a former hostage of the Colombian rebels, is a lifelong missionary to that same group in the jungles of Colombia. He is an influential friend to military and government leaders in Colombia, Cuba, Mexico, Venezuela, and the United States. Russell's ministry shares the gospel via twelve radio stations, hundreds of thousands of Bibles, books, and movies distributed through airplane parachute drops, and via numerous speaking engagements for groups of leaders, prisoners, and individuals. Russell goes wherever the Lord leads, whether it's to speak with a president or to go deep into the jungle to help an individual in trouble. He has witnessed thousands commit their lives to Christ.

Receive regular newsletter updates: http://eepurl.com/qmazf

American bush pilot Russell Stendal, on routine business, landed his plane in a remote Colombian village. Gunfire exploded throughout the town and within minutes Russell's 142 day ordeal had begun. The Colombian cartel explained that this was a kidnapping for ransom and that he would be held until payment was made.

Held at gunpoint deep in the jungle and with little else to occupy his time, Russell got ahold of some paper and began to write. He told the story of his life and kept a record of his experience in the guerrilla camp. His "book" became a bridge to the men who held him hostage and now serves as the basis for this incredible true story of how God's love penetrated a physical and ideological jungle.

"My captors tied me up and left the rope on day and night. They were seriously trying to completely break me psychologically and then brainwash me. Every day new things were done to alter me and work towards that goal. My captors started telling me scare stories. Some of these stories were about wild animals. They told me some of the wildest, hair-raising tales about lions and tigers that I have ever heard. These stories were designed both to intimidate me, reducing my ability to sleep, and to cause me to think twice before I decided to try to escape into the jungle again."

This world is in a state of constant unrest, but we must not be distracted from what God is doing now and in the future. God is patient, but soon He will restore His chosen people to a right relationship with Him, though this comes at a cost. All humanity will be affected. Your world will be changed in unprecedented ways and drinking from the River of God is the only answer.

The River of God opens with the river in the Garden of Eden, defines God's plans through biblical prophecy, numerology, and typology, and culminates in Revelation with the pure river of life proceeding from the throne of God for His people. Are you ready to stand firm during the coming tumultuous times? Discover your strength in the waters that flow from the River of God.

jubilee
B I B L E   2000

*Hear what God is
saying through this
original translation*

ANEKO Press